USA TODAY

Lifeline

BIOGRAPHIES

STEPHENIE MEYER

Dreaming of *Twilight*

by Katherine Krohn

T|F

For Sheggy, who brought me soup when I needed it most

Twenty-First Century Books
A division of Lerner Publishing Group, Inc.
241 First Avenue North
Minneapolis, MN 55401 U.S.A.

Website address: www.lernerbooks.com

Library of Congress Cataloging-in-Publication Data

Krohn, Katherine E.
    Stephenie Meyer : dreaming of *Twilight* / by Katherine Krohn.
       p.   cm. — (USA today lifeline biographies)
    Includes bibliographical references and index.
    ISBN 978-0-7613-5220-4 (lib. bdg. : alk. paper)
    1. Meyer, Stephenie, 1973– —Juvenile literature. 2. Authors, American—21st century—Biography—Juvenile literature. 3. Young adult fiction—Authorship—Juvenile literature. I. Title. II. Title: Dreaming of Twilight.
PS3613.E979Z75 2011
813'.6—dc22 [B]   2010001425

Manufactured in the United States of America
2 – VI – 3/1/11

USA TODAY | Lifeline
BIOGRAPHIES

First-time author: Stephenie Meyer wrote the book *Twilight* in three months, after having a vivid dream about a vampire in love with a human girl.

Fame Dawns

In the fall of 2003, a stay-at-home mom named Stephenie Meyer jumped for joy in her Phoenix, Arizona, home. She shrieked again and again. A New York publisher, Little, Brown, wanted to publish her first attempt at writing, a manuscript titled *Twilight*. She couldn't believe it!

Not only did the publisher want to publish the book but also two sequels (follow-up books that continue the story). Meyer signed a three-book deal (she later added a fourth book), and a publishing phenomenon known as the *Twilight* saga was born.

One night, just three months earlier, Meyer had had a vivid dream. In the dream, a teenage boy and girl were standing in a meadow, talking. The boy and girl were in love, but the pair had an unusual predicament.

The girl was a normal human teenager. She was shy and a little awkward. The boy was quite different. On the surface, he appeared to be an unusually handsome seventeen-year-old with a concerned and sober demeanor. But in reality, he was a 107-year-old vampire, faced with the troublesome urge to drink the blood of this girl he loves.

When Meyer awoke the next morning, the dream stayed with her. She wanted to keep the dream alive and keep the characters alive, so she wrote it down. Later that day, she expanded on the scene in the meadow. As the story grew, more and more characters entered the plot. And she found names for the two main characters—Edward and Bella.

Despite the demands of raising three children under the age of five, Meyer continued to re-visit her vampire dream, and write and write. In only three months, she penned a complete manuscript.

Meyer's romantic *Twilight* has captured the attention of millions of fans around the world. *Twilight* and its sequels have been made into blockbuster movies, and

Best sellers: The books in Meyer's *Twilight* series have sold more than 80 million copies worldwide.

the formerly little-known mom from Phoenix is one of the richest women in the United States.

Meyer's *Twilight* has remained on *New York Times* best seller lists for more than two years. Almost 20 million copies of the book have been sold worldwide, and the book has been translated into more than thirty languages.

In the fall of 2008, the movie version of *Twilight* premiered. Directed by Catherine Hardwicke (director of *Thirteen* and other films geared toward a teenage audience), the film was a major box office draw.

In November 2009, zealous fans stood in long lines for hours to catch the premiere of *The Twilight Saga: New Moon*, the film version of the second book in the *Twilight* series. The film broke box office records, earning $350 million in its debut month alone.

Fan pandemonium: Actor Robert Pattinson, who plays Edward in the *Twilight* movies, signs autographs for fans at the premiere of *The Twilight Saga: New Moon* in Los Angeles, California, in November 2009.

Meyer's novels have inspired hundreds of Internet *Twilight* fan clubs, with names such as "Twi-hards," "Twi-lighters," and "Twi-moms." Groups hold *Twilight*-inspired parties and conventions. High schools across the United States hold *Twilight*-themed proms. Fans can purchase *Twilight*-inspired merchandise—everything from pajamas to key chains—in stores around the United States.

When Meyer makes a bookstore appearance, hundreds of fans—many of them screaming, crying, or trembling—show up to see the author. Despite her success and fame, Meyer is known for coming across as grounded, warm, and genuine.

Because of her large fan base and her phenomenal success story, some critics have called Stephenie Meyer the new J. K. Rowling (the author of the wildly popular Harry Potter books). But while Rowling's books are popular with both male and female readers, Meyer's readers are mostly females—of all ages.

"At our [library] branch, the predominant age has been middle [school] and high school females, although we've had quite a few adult

Harry Potter: Meyer has been compared to British author J. K. Rowling *(above)* because of the women's phenomenal success stories.

women in their 30's and 40's and above [requesting] the books as well," said Natasha F., a Portland, Oregon, librarian.

Meyer didn't write *Twilight* for a specific age group or category of reader. She originally wrote the story to entertain herself. So it's perhaps not surprising that many adult women like the *Twilight* series too.

"I liked *Twilight* . . . because I felt all the feelings that Bella went through," said a thirty-something fan. "I loved the romance," she added. "Made me want to be Bella, the plain, simple girl who is seen as the most beautiful girl—by the hottest, hard-to-get guy she's ever met."

Not everyone is a fan of Meyer's writings. But more often than not, those who like her books are passionate about them.

Deborah Brady, forty-eight, a middle school teacher from Minnesota, became a Stephenie Meyer fan after observing the particular way her female students (ages twelve and thirteen) carried their copies of *Twilight*. "I see a lot of girls holding big fat books," said Brady, "but it was the way they were *clutching* that particular book that got

Passionate readers: Young fans pore over bookstore copies of *Twilight*.

me sucked in, that made me want to read it. I needed to know what was exciting them about this book."

Meyer's *Twilight* series has fueled the young adult, or YA, book industry. In November 2009, television host Oprah Winfrey noted on her program, *The Oprah Winfrey Show*, that Meyer has helped create a "culture of literacy" in many middle and high schools. In other words, Meyer's books have gotten kids reading.

"I do think that she's helped inspire kids to read, much in the same way Harry Potter did," says Natasha F., a youth librarian in a public library. "She has the talent to engulf you in her story and put you on the scene of it," agrees fan Alesha Lurie, a cashier in Oregon.

Stephenie Meyer didn't expect fame—or even to be published—when she began writing *Twilight*. Since her spectacular rise to publishing success, her life has changed dramatically. She's had what she calls "a crazy, rollercoaster-sans [without]-seatbelts experience from the very beginning." But Meyer has also found something satisfying and priceless—her calling as a writer.

Phoenix: Stephenie moved with her family to Phoenix, Arizona, when she was four years old. A new housing development in Phoenix is shown in this photo from 1977.

Girlhood

On December 24, 1973, a baby girl with bright eyes and thick, dark hair was born to Candy and Stephen Morgan of Hartford, Connecticut. They decided to name the baby after her father, adding an "ie" to the name Stephen. Stephenie had an older sister, Emily. And before long, Stephenie's younger sister, Heidi, was born. In the years to follow, brothers Jacob, Seth, and Paul joined the family.

Meyer has used all her siblings' names for characters in the *Twilight* saga. In the novels, Jacob is the heroine Bella's friend. Emily, Seth, and Paul belong to Jacob's Native American tribe. Heidi is a vampire who appears later in the saga.

Stephen Morgan worked as an executive at a contracting firm. Her mother was a stay-at-home mom, running a busy household. Stephenie's family moved to the Phoenix, Arizona, area when she was four.

Phoenix, nicknamed the Valley of the Sun, had approximately 600,000 residents in the mid-1970s. (Since that time, the population has nearly doubled.) Phoenix attracted many visitors, as well as new residents, drawn to the sunny city. Stephenie's family lived in Scottsdale, one of the cities in the thriving, fast-growing metropolitan area.

Faithful Daughter

Stephenie's parents had strong religious faith and passed their beliefs on to their children. They belonged to the Church of Jesus Christ of Latter-day Saints (LDS). The LDS Church is part of the Mormon religion, and LDS members are often called Mormons. The LDS Church was

Worldwide, the LDS Church has about 13 million members. About 5.5 million live in the United States. About 66 percent of U.S. Mormons live in Utah. About 4 percent live in Meyer's home state of Arizona.

founded by Joseph Smith Jr. in New York State in 1830. Stephenie's family attended church services regularly. They were active members of their religious community.

The LDS Church encourages Mormon families to set aside what is called family home evenings. On these nights, the family stays in to play games, eat favorite treats, and engage in other fun activities. It is also a time for the family to pray together and reflect on the teachings of their religion.

The Meyer family enjoyed spending time together. Stephenie and her family were very close.

Mormon leader: Joseph Smith Jr. (1805–1844), shown in a detail of this photo, founded the Church of Jesus Christ of Latter-day Saints. Members of the church are called Mormons.

Because Stephenie was the second-oldest child, she helped her parents look after her younger brothers and sister.

Stephen and Candy Morgan taught their children to observe and obey the LDS beliefs. For example, the religion discourages all members from consuming coffee, tea, alcohol, and tobacco. In some families, television watching is not encouraged. Parents monitor children's Internet usage and music selections. Children as well as adults can only watch movies with G or PG-13 ratings. Rules about dating are strictly enforced. Intimate physical relationships outside of marriage are forbidden.

Family time: This Mormon family reads aloud. Family home evenings are an important part of the LDS Church's teachings.

Later in her life, Stephenie told a reporter that she appreciated the strict way she was raised. She felt that her parents' careful guidance provided a safe, carefree environment. "I got to be a child for a really long time," said Stephenie.

A House Full of Books

Stephenie's parents loved books. They taught their children to love books too. They often read aloud to Stephenie and her brothers and sisters. In 1980, when Stephenie was seven, her father read his children *The Sword of Shannara* as a bedtime story. This novel by Terry Brooks is a fantasy epic similar to J. R. R. Tolkien's *The Lord of the Rings*. The story is set on Earth after a nuclear war—a world in which humans, gnomes, elves, and warlocks reside. Just when Stephen got to a dramatic moment in the story, he would bookmark the page, close the book, and tell the children that it was time for bed. Reluctantly, the kids would go to bed, wondering what was going to happen next in the enthralling tale.

Each day, Stephenie would sneak the book out of its hiding place in her parents' closet. She started reading where her dad left off the night before. At the time, Stephenie didn't know that the book was written for adults. And she didn't know that she was reading far beyond a normal second-grade reading level. She just knew that the story was exciting and she had to find out what would happen next.

When her father finished reading his children *The Sword of Shannara*, Stephenie reread the whole book herself. It was the first big book she had ever read. She liked it so well that she read it over and over again—ten times that year! Stephenie was excited when Terry Brooks added two more books to the series. She loved how a good book could carry her away, in a sense, to a whole new world.

Favorite book: Author Margaret Mitchell *(above)* published *Gone with the Wind* in 1936. Stephenie's father read the novel to his children at bedtime.

The next year, when Stephenie was eight, her father read the kids *Gone with the Wind*. Written for adults, Margaret Mitchell's novel is an epic romance set in the American South. It takes place in the 1860s, during the Civil War era. Stephenie looked forward to hearing her dad read a new chapter from the book each night. As with *The*

Sword of Shannara, Stephenie couldn't wait until the following evening to see what was going to happen next. Each morning, she got the heavy book off the shelf and read ahead in the story.

The Reader

By the time she was nine, Stephenie's family had nicknamed her the reader. When Stephenie wasn't at school or outside playing, she was often seen with a thick book in her hands. As she read, her long, wavy hair cascaded over her face, creating a wall of privacy between her and the rest of the world.

Stephenie loved to lose herself in a world created by a talented author. When Stephenie saw her parents read, it inspired her to read too. "There is something about seeing your Dad, who you know is a very, very busy person, and you know how much his time counts, and when you see him unable to rip himself away from a book, it impacts you," Stephenie told interviewer Nancy Pearl in 2007.

Stephenie's parents' bookshelf was her first library. Stephenie read the books that her parents read. Stephen Morgan preferred science fiction and fantasy, including Terry Brooks's writing and the works of Orson Scott Card. Candy Morgan gravitated toward classic romantic novels by authors such as Jane Austen and Charlotte Brontë.

Science fiction: Stephenie and her father read books by Orson Scott Card *(above)*. Card is an author and political activist, as well as a Mormon like Stephenie's family.

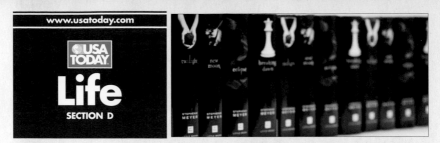

www.usatoday.com

USA TODAY

Life
SECTION D

October 28, 1999

Our love affair with Jane Austen

<u>From the Pages of</u>
<u>USA TODAY</u>

With her perfect dialogue, unforgettable characters and laser-sharp insight into the minds and hearts of human beings, Jane Austen today rules from beyond the grave she entered in 1817 at age 41. Her stories of love being found or lost within the confines of a rigid society resonate deeply in these times of casual hookups and dating techniques best suited for the mosh pit.

"Her characters don't change to get the guy," says Romance Classics [from 1997–2000, a part of the WE cable television channel] general manager Martin von Ruden. Austen's heroines are "hopeful, romantic women. They get men on their own terms."

—Deirdre Donahue

Jane Austen

Stephenie especially enjoyed stories told from the heroine's point of view. One of her favorite books was Jane Austen's *Pride and Prejudice*. This 1813 novel focuses on Elizabeth Bennett, a young woman living with her parents and four sisters in England in the early 1800s.

The story of *Jane Eyre* also captivated Stephenie. The book, written by Charlotte Brontë, was published in England in 1847. The tale is told from the perspective of Jane, an orphan who meets with many hardships but eventually finds love.

For young Stephenie, Jane Eyre was not just a character but a real person. Stephenie read the book again and again. "Jane was someone I was close to as a child," said Stephenie. "We were good friends! I think in some ways she was more real to me than any other fictional heroine."

Stephenie also loved the *Anne of Green Gables* series by Lucy Maud Montgomery. The first book in the series, *Anne of Green Gables*, was published in 1908. The story begins in the 1800s on Canada's Prince Edward Island. Middle-aged siblings Marilla and Matthew Cuthbert decide to adopt a boy to work on their farm. But instead, the orphanage sends eleven-year-old Anne Shirley. Anne is bright and chatty and has a vivid imagination. At first, Anne's talkative nature is almost too much for Marilla. But the Cuthberts decide to keep the child and

Childhood favorite: As a child, Stephenie enjoyed reading books by Lucy Maud Montgomery *(above)*.

quickly grow to love her. Each book in the series recounts a phase of Anne's life, including her childhood, teenage years, her marriage, and the birth of her first child. "We got the whole life, and I loved that," Stephenie later said of the books.

Stephenie's other favorite authors included English playwright William Shakespeare, Irish author Maeve Binchy, British novelist Daphne du Maurier, and American novelist Louisa May Alcott. She especially liked Alcott's *Little Women* series, about four sisters growing up together in nineteenth-century Massachusetts. Stephenie identified with the character Jo in the books. Jo is a bit of a tomboy, is very smart, and likes to read and write.

In sixth grade, Stephenie started at Cocopah Middle School. The attractive, modern-looking, redbrick school stood on East Cholla Street in Scottsdale. Cocopah's school colors were blue and gold, and the school mascot was the mustang (a type of horse). Stephenie was a good student. Her favorite subject was English, mainly because she loved words and books. Each day when she got home from school, she headed to her room to read.

On Wednesdays, Stephenie visited the library to check out a new book for the week. When she scanned the bookshelves, she sought out the thickest, fattest book she could find.

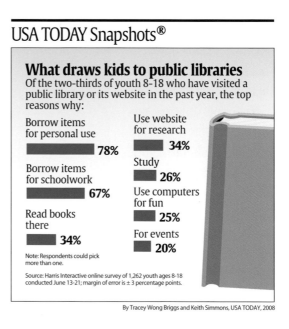

USA TODAY Snapshots®

What draws kids to public libraries

Of the two-thirds of youth 8-18 who have visited a public library or its website in the past year, the top reasons why:

Borrow items for personal use
78%

Borrow items for schoolwork
67%

Read books there
34%

Use website for research
34%

Study
26%

Use computers for fun
25%

For events
20%

Note: Respondents could pick more than one.

Source: Harris Interactive online survey of 1,262 youth ages 8-18 conducted June 13-21; margin of error is ± 3 percentage points.

By Tracey Wong Briggs and Keith Simmons, USA TODAY, 2008

Late Bloomer

In 1987 Stephenie entered high school. She attended Chaparral High School in Scottsdale. Chaparral High is known for being one of the best academic schools in Arizona.

Many students at Stephenie's school came from well-to-do families. A lot of the kids drove expensive cars and had plenty of spending money. Stephenie's family had enough money, and she and her siblings had the things they needed. But the Morgans weren't rich.

When Stephenie compared herself to the other kids, especially the popular girls, she sometimes felt like a misfit. She even

Sister act: Stephenie *(right)* and her older sister, Emily, pose in a photo from their high school yearbook. Stephenie enjoyed spending time with her family when she was in high school.

felt that she looked different. Many of her classmates had deep tans from the Phoenix sun, but Stephenie's skin was naturally fair. She had friends, but she wasn't a part of the popular crowd. And she preferred reading and spending time with her family to dating.

When Stephenie did date, it really meant something to her. "I was a late bloomer," said Stephenie. "When I was sixteen, holding hands was just—wow."

Stephenie knew that some girls her age were experimenting with sex. Stephenie couldn't relate to them. Instead, she identified more with literary characters from other eras—girls such as Elizabeth Bennett and Jane Eyre. Just as she had each year since she was a young girl, Stephenie reread her favorite novels, paying her fictional friends a visit once again.

Coming of Age

Stephenie's parents encouraged all their children to take their schoolwork seriously. The Morgan children were expected to study hard and do their best. Stephenie was fortunate. Learning came easily to her, and she earned top grades. In 1991, Stephenie's senior year, she was awarded a scholarship to Brigham Young University. The acclaimed university in Provo, Utah, was founded by members of the LDS Church.

Stephenie decided to major in English at college. Some of her friends teased her. They said that if she majored in English, she wouldn't be able to get a job after graduation. There was no money in being an English major, they said. But Stephenie didn't care what

Senior year: Stephenie did well in high school and was awarded a college scholarship her senior year.

College life: Stephenie attended Brigham Young University in Provo, Utah. She decided to major in English.

anybody said. She loved literature and reading. She was following her heart.

During college, Stephenie shared an apartment with six female friends. She liked living with lots of young women. She thought of them as her sisters, similar to the family of close sisters in *Little Women*. It was

USA TODAY Snapshots®

Sizing up private universities

Private, non-profit colleges and universities with the largest single-campus enrollment[1]:

New York University, New York City
👤👤👤👤👤👤👤👤👤👤👤👤👤👤👤👤👤👤👤👤 **40,004**

Brigham Young University, Provo, Utah
👤👤👤👤👤👤👤👤👤👤👤👤👤👤👤👤👤 **34,067**

University of Southern California, Los Angeles
👤👤👤👤👤👤👤👤👤👤👤👤👤👤👤👤 **32,836**

Boston University
👤👤👤👤👤👤👤👤👤👤👤👤👤👤👤 **30,957**

Harvard University, Cambridge, Mass.
👤👤👤👤👤👤👤👤👤👤👤👤 **25,017**

George Washington University, Washington, D.C.
👤👤👤👤👤👤👤👤👤👤👤👤 **24,099**

1 – Data are from fall 2005
Source: American Council on Education, data from the U.S. Department of Education

By Tracy Wong Briggs and Karl Gelles, USA TODAY, 2007

fun swapping clothes with her six roommates. And sometimes they would stay up all night, just talking and laughing.

In the summer of 1993, Stephenie returned home to Phoenix to visit her family. While there, she ran into a young man she had known since childhood. His name was Christian Meyer, but everybody called him Pancho. She recognized him from weekly church activities. She had seen him around for years, but she had never actually talked to him. In fact, she hadn't really liked Pancho when they were growing up. He hung out with a different crowd of friends, and she found some of those friends a little mean.

As Stephenie and Pancho talked, her perceptions of him changed. Pancho had recently returned from an LDS church mission to Chile. As Pancho told Stephenie about the experience, she watched his face. He had turned into a handsome man. Brown-haired Pancho had a nice smile. He was easygoing, friendly, and caring toward others. Stephenie realized that she really liked him.

A couple: Stephenie and her husband, Pancho Meyer, are shown here in 2008.

USA TODAY
Life
SECTION D

October 21, 1997

Mormons on mission to grow

<u>From the Pages of</u>
<u>USA TODAY</u>

In 1980, sociologist Rodney Stark ran some numbers and made a prediction. During the next hundred years, he said, the Church of Jesus Christ of Latter-day Saints—better known as the Mormon Church—would grow 40% a decade.

Sixteen years later, he turned back to his tables and found he had been wrong.

"They've been doing about 50%," says Stark. "They're a million ahead of the largest projections."

Last year, 78,000 children of members and 330,000 converts were baptized. In November, membership will hit 10 million. If the 167-year-old church expands according to projections, it will have 260 million members by 2080. It would then "be counted as one of the five or six big world religions," Stark says.

Church membership in the USA, the Philippines, and Central and South America is growing at warp speed. In part, the reason is missionaries: About 56,000 of them are now working in 161 countries.

At 19, "worthy" [that is, meeting church standards] men spend about two years as missionaries. Women who go do so at 21, serving for 18 months.

The missionaries work hard, but most conversions are inspired by others. "People join because their family members or good friends are members. . . . That's the way movements always grow," Stark says.

—Katy Kelly

Mormon missionaries in Tonga, islands in the southwest Pacific Ocean

Pancho was immediately attracted to Stephenie too. She was a natural beauty, with big brown eyes and long, lustrous hair. Pancho also liked that Stephenie was kind, sincere, and friendly. Pancho asked Stephenie out on a date. Because of her religious beliefs, Stephenie needed her parents' approval before dating anyone. Stephen and Candy approved of Pancho as a suitor for their daughter. After all, they had known Pancho's parents for years. Both families went to the same church.

Stephenie and Pancho quickly fell in love. In 1994, within nine months of their first conversation, Stephenie and Pancho married. Stephenie Morgan became Stephenie Meyer.

Meyer was a little sad to leave her apartment and her roommates. She knew she would miss having her friends around. But she loved Pancho and was excited to start her married life. The next year, 1995, Meyer graduated from Brigham Young University with a degree in English. She took a job as a receptionist for a real estate property company. Pancho got a job as an accountant. They moved into an adobe-style house near her parents' home in Scottsdale. Meyer was happy to be living near her family once again.

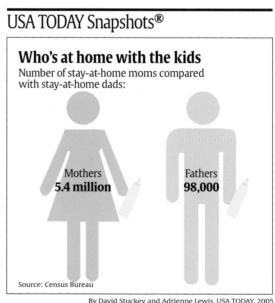

USA TODAY Snapshots®

Who's at home with the kids

Number of stay-at-home moms compared with stay-at-home dads:

Mothers
5.4 million

Fathers
98,000

Source: Census Bureau

By David Stuckey and Adrienne Lewis, USA TODAY, 2005

In 1997 Stephenie and Pancho Meyer had their first child, Gabriel. They called him Gabe for short. Meyer soon quit her job to care for her new son full-time. "Once I had Gabe, I just wanted to be his mom," said Meyer.

Three years later, the Meyers added another child to their family, a boy named Seth. Baby Eli was born two years later. "When I was younger I wanted to be just like Jo March [of *Little Women*] and have [all] boys," Meyer said in a 2007 interview, "and when I was older I wanted all girls. . . . I got my first wish."

Writer's dream: The idea for *Twilight* started with a dream Stephenie had. She dreamed about a couple in a meadow. Later, meadow scenes appeared in both the movies *Twilight* and *The Twilight Saga: New Moon* (*shown here*).

Dreaming of *Twilight*

Meyer had lots of creative energy and imagination. She liked to make her kids' Halloween costumes. She also enjoyed scrapbooking. It was fun to paste photos and an assortment of mementos from family events and activities into an attractive book. She enjoyed making something special and lasting.

Several years earlier, Meyer had tried writing. Various ideas for stories had come to her, and she had started a couple of short stories. But the projects didn't go far.

She had put them away in a drawer and forgotten about them.

Though she was a very creative person, most of Meyer's energy went into being a mom to Gabe, Seth, and Eli. For the most part, Meyer put her own needs—and her imagination—aside.

Passion and Frenzy

On the evening of June 1, 2003, Meyer checked on her kids, turned off the lights, and got ready for bed. Pancho had a head cold. Because she didn't want to catch Pancho's cold, Meyer decided to sleep in the guest room. Exhausted from a long day, she soon fell into a deep slumber.

That night Meyer had a dream that was unusually vivid and vibrant. In the dream, a teenage girl and boy were having a conversation in a meadow. The girl was an ordinary human. The boy was a vampire,

IN FOCUS

Dreams and Imagination

Why do ideas and inspirations sometime come to us when we dream? Is there a part of the brain where our creativity is centered, and is it somehow activated when we "let go" and sleep?

Scientists have tried to understand dreams and dreaming for many years. "Dreaming is so basic to human existence, it's astonishing we don't understand it better," wrote Jay Dixit in *Psychology Today*. "It consumes years of our lives, and no other single activity exerts such a powerful pull on our imaginations. Yet central as dreaming is, we still have no idea why we dream."

Sometimes dreams bring us deep inspiration, as with Meyer's dream about the couple in the meadow. The 1965 song "Yesterday" also came to former Beatle Paul McCartney in a dream. As *Time* magazine reporter Lev Grossman said, "Sometimes you have the dream, and sometimes the dream has you."

whose pale white skin sparkled like diamonds in the open sun of the meadow. The feelings in the dream—the emotions of the boy and girl—were vivid to Meyer too. The girl loved the boy. She was in awe of him and his beauty. Though she knew he was very dangerous, she didn't want to lose him. The boy loved the girl too. But his desire to love her was matched by his desire to kill her. In her dream, Meyer could feel the emotional struggle within the boy.

When Meyer opened her eyes the next morning, the dream stayed with her. She lay in bed for a while, just thinking about the dream, the young couple, and their strange and compelling predicament. "Where would it go next?" she wondered. "Would he kill her, or would they work it out?"

When she heard her kids and husband talking, she got out of bed. She knew she had countless tasks ahead of her that day. She had to make the kids breakfast. Then she had to get them dressed and drive them to swimming lessons. She was in the middle of potty training the baby. When she looked at her calendar, she also realized that she planned to start a diet that day. But even as she went about her busy routine, the vampire dream flashed through her mind. It was almost as if the dream—or the characters in the dream—weren't going to let her forget it.

Later that day, Meyer had a few minutes to herself. She went to the family computer and wrote down as much of the dream as she could remember. Occasionally she'd get up to give one of the children juice or a snack, or to change a diaper. But when she finished each task, she returned to the computer, taking notes on the scene in the meadow. After her family went to bed that night, she got on the computer again. It was much easier to write when the house was quiet and there were no interruptions.

When Meyer thought of the vampire boy in her dream, she felt as though she understood him. It was as if the character of the vampire had been given to her in the dream—laid out for her—and she just needed to write the details down before they slipped away.

Night owl: Stephenie would work on the book while her husband and children were asleep at night.

In the back of her mind, Meyer wasn't sure why she was bothering to write. She hadn't written anything in so long. And she had certainly never thought of herself as an author. Meyer's writing was sketchy and slow at first. But as she pushed her self-doubt out of the way, the writing began to flow faster and faster. She began to write with a "passion and frenzy" about the scene in the meadow. (That scene would eventually become chapter 13 of *Twilight*.)

At first she didn't have names for the two main characters, so she referred to them as "he" and "she." She didn't make an outline or plan the plot. She was simply telling herself a story. She could take her characters where she wanted them to go, and she was compelled to find out what would happen next. "It was this wonderful experience, and I really had always thought that reading was the best thing," said Meyer. "And then I discovered that day that writing was just a little bit better."

Before Meyer went to bed that night, she had written ten single-spaced pages of text. The next night, she wrote again, expanding on the scene in the meadow. The teenage girl in the dream was beginning to take shape in her mind. For example, the girl was a little shy and a bit awkward but very intelligent. Each night Meyer wrote more. The writing came fast. "On a good day I would write 10 or 12 pages, single-spaced. That's a good chapter and then some," said Meyer.

Sometimes ideas came to Meyer at night when she slept. She kept a notebook by her bed to jot down new ideas so she wouldn't forget them. Whenever she got a free moment during the day, she worked on her story. Without an outline, Meyer simply worked forward from the scene in her dream. She filled in details and added characters, until she reached the conclusion of the story. Then she went back and created the beginning of the story and wrote up to the scene in the meadow.

Naming the Characters

Meyer knew she couldn't call her lead characters "he" and "she" for-ever. They needed names. For the role of the vampire, Meyer wanted a name that sounded old-fashioned, had a romantic tone to it, and wasn't used too much anymore. She decided on the name Edward.

In the story, Edward appears as a teenager. But he is really a 107-year-old vampire, born on June 20, 1901. In 1918 Edward fell ill with a serious form of influenza. The 1918 influenza pandemic was a real historical event that killed millions of people worldwide.

A pandemic is a disease outbreak that spreads over a large area and affects a large part of the population. The 1918 influenza pandemic spread around the world and lasted into 1919. About 500 million people, or one-third of the world's population, fell ill. Researchers are not sure how many people died in the pandemic. But recent estimates stand at 30 to 50 million. That includes about 675,000 Americans.

The Cullen Clan

In *Twilight*, Bella Swan is drawn into the lives of Edward's family members. The Cullens are listed below.

Alice Cullen: Carlisle and Esme's adopted daughter and adoptive sister of Edward, Rosalie, and Emmett. She is married to Jasper.

Dr. Carlisle Cullen: Edward's adoptive father and a vampire. Carlisle works as a physician at the local hospital.

Edward Cullen: A century-old vampire posing as a high school student. Edward is also Bella's main love interest.

Emmett Cullen: Rosalie's husband and adoptive brother of Edward, Alice, and Jasper.

Esme Cullen: Carlisle's wife and the adoptive mother of Edward, Rosalie, Emmett, Jasper, and Alice

Jasper Hale: Carlisle and Esme's adopted son. He is the adoptive brother of Edward, Emmett, and Rosalie. Jasper is married to Alice.

Rosalie Hale: Carlisle and Esme's adopted daughter. She is the adoptive sister of Edward, Alice, and Jasper, and is married to Emmett.

Cullen cast: The Cullen family from the movie version of *Twilight (left to right)*: Kellan Lutz (Emmett), Nikki Reed (Rosalie), Elizabeth Reaser (Esme), Robert Pattinson (Edward), Peter Facinelli (Carlisle), Ashley Greene (Alice), and Jackson Rathbone (Jasper).

Unknown to Edward, his doctor, Carlisle Cullen, was a vampire. But Cullen was a benevolent, or well-meaning, vampire. As Edward lay dying, Cullen bit him so that he wouldn't die permanently. Edward becomes seventeen forever on that day. He takes the last name of Cullen.

Dr. Cullen had been turned into a vampire in England in the 1700s. In choosing the surname for the character, Meyer looked through lists of people who had died in Great Britain in the 1700s. The surname Cullen just seemed right, thought Meyer.

Meyer wanted a special name for the shy and sensitive human girl who falls in love with Edward. Meyer had set aside the name Isabella (Bella for short) in case she ever gave birth to a baby girl. But after having three children, Meyer and Pancho made a decision to not have any more. Meyer decided to give her heroine the name she had saved for her own daughter. She chose Swan as Bella's last name. The name sounded romantic to Meyer, reminding her of the fairy tale of the ugly duckling that transforms into a beautiful swan.

Meyer did research to invent other characters' names. For example, to name Edward's brother, Jasper, she researched first and last names of soldiers who had fought for the Confederate (Southern) army in the American Civil War. She searched old census records, looking for names that were popular at the time the character was born. She named some characters after her brothers and sisters. Meyer also selected names by flipping through the phone book and making note of interesting names.

While she wrote, Meyer wasn't thinking about who was going to be reading her story. In other words, she didn't make her main characters teenagers because she was writing for a young adult audience. She was writing the story for herself, and the couple in her dream happened to be seventeen-year-olds. But Meyer thought the time frame of high school was perfect for her story. "It's the first time you fall in love, it's the first time you kiss somebody. All those feelings are so much stronger," Meyer told a reporter from the *Times*, a British newspaper. "You are not calloused yet, you haven't had your heart broken a few times so you know how to handle it.

Everything is very vivid so it's a lot of fun to write about."

Meyer did a Google search to choose the setting for her story. She wanted a place where it rained a lot—a place that would impart a moody, cool, and cloudy feeling. It was important that the story take place in a beautiful natural setting too—near acres and acres of deep forest. Meyer chose Forks, Washington, in the state's Olympic rain forest. The rain forest is not far from the Pacific Ocean coast. She titled her work-in-progress "Forks."

Rain forest: Water from storms off the Pacific Ocean feed Washington's Olympic rain forest. The forest is home to large trees, moss, ferns, and a large variety of wildlife.

Sometimes details of her life worked their way into Meyer's writing. In an early scene, Bella is in biology class and gets woozy at the sight of blood. She has to leave class and visit the school nurse. In real life, when Meyer was a high school student, she once passed out during biology class.

IN F⊕CUS

Meyer's Vampires

While writing *Twilight*, Meyer did very little research on vampires. "The only time I really did ... was when the character Bella did research on vampires," said Meyer. "Because I was creating my own world, I didn't want to find out just how many rules I was breaking."

Before working on her story, Meyer had never read Bram Stoker's 1897 novel *Dracula*. She had never seen a Dracula movie or even the television show *Buffy the Vampire Slayer*. She had read some of Anne Rice's vampire novels in college when they were popular. But she really wasn't interested in horror fiction. She had never imagined that she would one day be writing books about vampires.

Because of her limited experience with the subject, Meyer felt free to create her own unique version of a vampire. Edward's coven (group) of vampires all have unique powers. Edward can read thoughts—everyone's thoughts except Bella's, that is. And Edward's sister Alice can see the future.

Some fictional vampires cannot tolerate sunlight, so they sleep in coffins during the day. But Edward simply avoids the sunlight. If he does go out in bright sun, he sparkles. Some classic vampires, such as Dracula, can be killed with a stake through the heart. Edward and his clan cannot be easily killed. They have superpowers and superstrength, and they can even fly.

Meyer often held her one-year-old baby, Eli, in her lap while she worked. "He's kind of a monkey, so he could cling, and I could type around him," Meyer told TV talk-show host Ellen DeGeneres in 2008. The baby would peek through Meyer's arms and watch *Blue's Clues* (a children's TV program on the Nickelodeon channel) while she worked.

Finding Her Passion

As a young girl, Meyer hadn't listened to much music. She had adored the world of books instead. As an adult, Meyer was finding her passion for music.

When she worked on "Forks," she discovered that music made a great accompaniment to her writing. She liked many bands and performing artists, but she particularly enjoyed the band Muse. A muse is a source of inspiration, and Meyer found that the band lived up to its name. "They universally work for my writing style," she said. "If I have to write a scene of despair, 'Apocalypse Please' [a Muse song] will work. And if I have to write an action scene, I can put on 'Assassin.' If I have to write a scene about love, 'Starlight' will work. They have so many emotions!"

Each day Meyer sat in front of the computer for hours. Sometimes she typed well into the night. Pancho grew frustrated. "You never sleep, you don't talk to me, I never get to use the computer," he complained. "*What* are you doing?[2]

Meyer didn't want to tell Pancho that she was writing a story about vampires. She figured he'd just think it was weird. "I'm just messing around with something," she told him, trying to sound casual.

In truth, Meyer was having fun. The process was exciting, "like reading the best book ever, but you were in charge," said Meyer. And she was allowing herself to be creative for the first time in years, it seemed. The experience was gratifying. Not only was she creating a make-believe world, but she felt as if she was reconnecting with another part of herself.

Muse is a rock band from Devon, a region in southwestern England. Founded in 1994, Muse includes Matthew Bellamy, Christopher Wolstenholme, and Dominic Howard.

Writing process: Meyer spent much of her free time working on *Twilight*. She decided to write the story from the heroine's perspective.

The Story Unfolds

Meyer had always preferred books told from the perspective of the heroine. She wrote her book from the point of view of seventeen-year-old Bella Swan.

Bella is a high school junior who reluctantly leaves sunny Arizona. She moves to the logging town of Forks, Washington, to live with her father, Charlie. (Her parents are divorced.) On the first day in her new school, Bella spies Edward Cullen and his siblings in the school cafeteria. Bella keeps glancing over at Edward's table, and a new school friend notices. The friend tells Bella that she shouldn't waste her time. Edward isn't interested in any of the girls at the school, says the friend.

When Bella gets to her biology class that day, she sees that Edward is in her class. The seat next to him at the lab table is empty, and Bella heads toward it. But as she comes closer, Edward appears to be revolted by her. He moves as far as he can from her at their lab table. He grits his teeth and clenches his fists. Bella is hurt and offended by Edward's behavior. She discreetly smells her armpits, checking for body odor. She wonders, why is he acting so repulsed? In reality, Edward is passionately attracted to Bella. He can smell her blood, and he has to fight his desire to kill her.

Edward is an unusual vampire. He and his family have made the choice to not take human life to satisfy their cravings for blood. Instead, they feed off animals that they hunt in the forest.

Father and daughter: *Twilight* centers around Bella moving to live with her dad in Forks, Washington, where she meets Edward. In a scene from *Twilight*, Edward (Robert Pattinson, *left*) talks with Bella (Kristen Stewart) and her father, Charlie (Billy Burke, *center*).

www.usatoday.com

USA TODAY

News

SECTION A

October 31, 1989

Vampires: A Fascination That Won't Die

From the Pages of
USA TODAY

The vampire lives.

The blood-drinking night stalker, part of worldwide mythology since ancient times, is more un-dead than ever. On any given night, the vampire—especially Count Dracula, the most famous of all—awaits willing victims in movie theaters, bookstores and video shops.

"The vampire is the charmer of the monster world," says novelist Anne Rice, explaining the fascination fed by her books, *Interview with the Vampire*, *The Vampire Lestat* and *Queen of the Damned*.

Dracula—the 1897 Bram Stoker novel that has inspired dozens of movies—still intrigues fans and scholars. Stoker's *Dracula* often is considered the source of modern vampire lore. But vampire myths started long before, says [Boston University professor Raymond] McNally, one of the world's leading authorities on vampire stories.

Actor Bela Lugosi as the title character in *Dracula* (1931)

"Human fascination with blood goes back to the beginning of recorded time. Primitive man saw that when the blood went out the life went out," he says. "The simple assumption was that by putting blood back in, you could put the life back in."

Making up vampire stories, [McNally] says, is a way of dealing with fear of death. "Everybody who loves life wants to live forever. But the problem is to live forever and stay young. To live forever and get old would be a bummer."

So vampires typically are beautiful, elegant beings who never age. But they also are tragic—they must hurt others to survive.

Rice's fans say the vampire's appeal is romance, "the promise that in the vampire's embrace they'd be transported out of the ordinary," she says. "He stands at the French windows and spreads his wings and promises to take you into his world."

—Kim Painter

Edward has learned to stave off his hunger pangs for human blood. But the smell of Bella's blood is so sweet and he is so drawn to her that he can barely control his instincts. His feelings are strong, unlike anything he has felt before.

As Meyer typed out her story, other important characters entered the scene. One was Jacob Black, a childhood friend of Bella. Jacob is a Native American of the Quileute Nation of western Washington (and like Edward, he has special powers). Bella's growing feelings for Edward and her sometimes confusing feelings for Jacob create a tension-filled love triangle. A tribe of human-killing vampires also enters the story, adding to the drama and danger that young Bella faces.

Movie love triangle: Costars *(left to right)* Taylor Lautner, Kristen Stewart, and Robert Pattinson play the roles of Jacob, Bella, and Edward in the *Twilight* movies. Fans of the books and movies feel very invested in the relationships among the characters.

> La Push, Washington, is home to the Quileute Native American Nation. The nation's ancient ancestors are among the oldest human inhabitants of the Pacific Northwest. According to legend, the first Quileutes were created by a supernatural figure called Q'wati (in English, "the transformer"), when Q'wati changed a wolf pack into humans.

Taking a Chance

Meyer usually kept in close touch with her siblings, especially her big sister, Emily. But since having her vivid vampire dream, she used all her spare time to write. Emily hadn't heard from Meyer for three whole weeks. She grew concerned. When Meyer finally returned her calls, Emily was full of questions.

"What's wrong? What happened?" asked Emily. "Are you alive?" At that point, Meyer knew it was time to tell someone what she was doing. She felt nervous to disclose her secret but excited too.

"Well, I'm kind of writing a story," said Meyer.

"So let me see it," said Emily. She was intrigued.

That day Meyer shared with her sister the stack of pages she had been writing. Emily was impressed. She thought the writing was good! And the story was compelling. She wanted to know what was going to happen next. Meyer agreed to send her each new section as she completed it.

As Meyer worked on the manuscript, Emily occasionally checked in and gave her sister encouragement. If she hadn't heard from Meyer for a few days, she prodded her writing along, asking when Meyer was going to send her a new section to read. Meanwhile, no one else in Meyer's family knew what she was working on—not even her husband.

Two months later, Meyer finished her manuscript. After Emily read the final chapter of the book, her mind was made up. "You've got to try and publish it," she demanded.

Meyer groaned. She didn't know the first thing about getting a book published, she said. And besides, who would want to publish it?

Writing the manuscript had been easy. But for Meyer, the idea of trying to get her manuscript published seemed scary and difficult, if not impossible.

Meyer's big sister was insistent. Emily thought Meyer's book was great. And she wasn't going to back down until Meyer took steps to seek out a publisher.

Meyer felt overwhelmed at the prospect of finding a publisher. But on the other hand, she *had* completed an entire manuscript. And it was long—130,000 words and twenty-four chapters. Meyer felt afraid, but her belief in her characters, along with a desire to keep her story alive, motivated her to move forward.

She wasn't sure how to get started. "I thought it worked like this: you printed a copy of your

Family support: Meyer *(above)* first told her older sister, Emily, about the story she was writing. Emily encouraged Meyer to try to get it published.

novel, wrapped it up in brown paper, and sent it off to a publishing house," said Meyer. "Ho ho ho, that's a good one."

As usual, when she had something to research, Meyer decided to do a Google search. She typed, "What do you do when you write a book?" Bit by bit, Meyer pieced together how to get a book published. First, she learned, she needed a literary agent. An agent represents authors' legal and financial interests and helps them find the right publishers. Meyer needed to find an agent who works with the type of book that she had written, she learned. She subscribed to WritersMarket.com (an online resource for new writers who want to be published) and learned about the various types of literary agents and publishers.

Over the next few days, Meyer decided to break the news to her whole family that she had written a book. When they heard how she had been spending her time, they were surprised. Meyer had written a book about vampires? Despite their surprise, her husband, parents,

Online tools: Meyer used the website WritersMarket.com to learn how to get a book published.

and siblings were all supportive. Meyer broke the news to friends too. While some were a little shocked at the subject matter of Meyer's book, they were proud of her. They encouraged her to move forward with her project.

Meyer's younger sister, Heidi, did some publishing research. She said that she had read on the website of popular writer Janet Evanovich that Writers House was a good literary agency. Meyer thought that since Evanovich is such a successful writer, she must know what she's talking about. Meyer sent a letter to Writers House and to fourteen other literary agencies.

Happiest Day of Her Life

With the "Forks" manuscript finished, Meyer had more time for her family and friends. In her spare time, she continued to write. She felt as though she wasn't ready to let go of her characters. She typed out several epilogues (follow-up stories) detailing what happens to the characters. She also began *Midnight Sun*, the *Twilight* story told from Edward Cullen's perspective.

Every day, Meyer checked her mailbox. Eventually a letter arrived from a literary agent. Meyer was thrilled. But it was a rejection letter. A few days later, another rejection arrived. And soon, another. In total, Meyer received nine rejection letters.

One day Meyer received a letter from Writers House, the first agent she had written to. She braced herself for yet another rejection. As she read the words of the letter, Meyer couldn't believe it. The agent wanted to see the first three chapters of her manuscript!

Meyer didn't know this, but the letter wasn't from an actual agent. It was from an assistant at Writers House, Genevieve. On a hunch, Genevieve had thought it worth the company's time to check out this unknown author, Stephenie Meyer, and her manuscript "Forks." Meyer mailed her the sample chapters and waited for her reply.

Several weeks later, Meyer got another letter from Writers House. As she opened the letter, her hands trembled with fear. It was

Difficult wait: After Meyer sent off her entire manuscript to Writers House, she had to wait weeks for a reply.

Genevieve again. She wrote that she loved the first three chapters of Meyer's book. For emphasis, Genevieve had gone back and underlined her words twice with a pen. She wanted Meyer to send her the rest of the manuscript. "That was the exact moment when I realized that I might actually see [the book] in print," recalled Meyer, "and really one of the happiest points in my whole life. I did a lot of screaming."

Without wasting another moment, Meyer printed out a fresh copy of her manuscript and mailed it to Writers House. For the next few days, Meyer waited in anticipation for a reply. She had plenty to do around the house and the needs of her kids were a big distraction, but still, she couldn't stop thinking about the manuscript she had submitted. What was going to happen? Was it possible that Writers House would actually like her manuscript? When Meyer didn't hear back from Genevieve for more than three weeks, she started to lose hope. Genevieve didn't like the book at all, Meyer thought to herself. Sure, maybe the first three chapters had caught her attention. But there must have been something wrong with the rest of the book, thought Meyer.

About a month after submitting her manuscript, Meyer got a call from Jodi Reamer, a literary agent at Writers House. Genevieve had shown Reamer the manuscript, and the agent loved it. Reamer explained to Meyer that Writers House wanted to represent her. As Meyer's agent, Reamer explained, she would send the manuscript to various publishers to see if there was any interest. "I tried really hard to sound professional and grown up during that conversation, but I'm not sure if I fooled her," said Meyer, on her official website.

For the next few weeks, Meyer and Reamer worked together to put the finishing touches on the manuscript. Reamer didn't like the title "Forks." The book was renamed *Twilight*. When she thought it was ready, Reamer mailed *Twilight* to nine publishers.

Meyer felt excited. But she still had her doubts. She wondered, would anyone really want to publish her book?

Literary agent: Jodi Reamer *(left),* seen here at the Surrey International Writers' Conference in Canada in 2004, works at Writers House. She is also an attorney.

Paying Off Her Minivan

On Thanksgiving weekend 2003, Boston, Massachusetts, publishing executive Megan Tingley boarded an airplane. Tingley worked for Little, Brown Books for Young Readers, a part of publisher Hachette Book Group USA. She had brought work to do on the long flight. She planned to read a hefty, six-hundred-page manuscript that had landed on her desk a few days earlier. As Tingley began reading, she was immediately drawn into the story. She flipped through the pages, wanting to know what was going to happen next. Tingley could barely believe how good the manuscript was. "I kept thinking, well, she can't possibly sustain this," recalled Tingley. "The whole book is going to fall apart. She's a first-time writer."

By the time her plane landed, Tingley had made up her mind. She wanted the book, and she wanted it desperately. Tingley left messages with Reamer, Meyer's agent. She also left messages with her colleagues at Little, Brown—she wanted to give them a heads-up. She had found a fantastic manuscript, and a significant deal was about to take place.

Making the deal: Megan Tingley, a publishing executive at Little, Brown Books for Young Readers, read Meyer's manuscript in 2003.

On the next business day, Tingley spoke with Reamer and offered her a financial deal. She said that not only did Little, Brown want *Twilight*, they wanted Meyer to write two sequels to the book. She offered to pay $300,000 for three books. Reamer was a shrewd agent. She had a feeling she could get more. She turned down Tingley's offer and asked for $1 million. By the end of the day, the publisher had offered Meyer a $750,000 advance—a huge amount for a first-time author—for three books. Reamer accepted the deal.

When Reamer called Meyer to tell her the good news, Meyer was flabbergasted. Seven hundred and fifty thousand dollars was far more than what she had expected. "I'd been hoping for $10,000 to pay off my minivan," Meyer said. She was thrilled.

Another book: Meyer started working on the second book in the *Twilight* series not long after signing her book deal.

Publishing Phenomenon

■■■■

Near the end of 2003, Meyer sat in front of her Macintosh computer at her marble desk in the family living area. She had signed a three-book deal with Little, Brown, so she had to get to work writing the first *Twilight* sequel. While she worked, she listened to music on her iPod headphones. Her kids played nearby.

One of the long epilogues that Meyer had written as soon as she finished *Twilight* gave her a head start on her second book, *New Moon*. Just as they had with her first book, the characters called her to the writing. Meyer cared about her characters. She felt as if they wanted to be heard, wanted their story told.

Twilight was slated to be released for publication in fall 2005. Meyer had a little more than a year to wait. In a way, that seemed like forever. On the other hand, she had lots of writing to do. And her publisher had told her that she'd soon have to travel and promote her books, especially if they were popular. Meyer knew that she needed time to adjust to the idea. She was going to be a published author.

Musical Muses

Just as she had during the writing of *Twilight*, she found that music helped her writing process while creating *New Moon*. Meyer listened to different music than she listened to when she wrote *Twilight*. She found that each scene in a story evoked, or demanded, its own special song or musical style.

While typing at her computer, she played songs by her favorite bands, such as Blue October, Motion City Soundtrack, Marjorie Fair and, of course, her favorite band, Muse.

Meyer's muse: Meyer likes to listen to rock band Muse *(above)*, as well as other bands, while she writes.

IN F☉CUS

Meyer's Musical Muses

Meyer has several musical muses. They change, depending on what she's working on. But dependable sources of inspiration include Linkin Park, the All-American Rejects, Coldplay, the Strokes, U2, My Chemical Romance, Travis, Brand New, Jimmy Eat World, Elbow, Weezer, and, of course, Muse.

Musical inspiration: The hard-driving music of Linkin Park uses elements of alternative metal and hip-hop. The band is shown here after winning a Grammy award in 2006.

When Meyer was writing an action scene, the band Linkin Park helped her with the rhythm and tempo of her writing. Sometimes she'd listen to a particular song, such as Linkin Park's "By Myself," over and over again, just letting it loop on her iPod.

Meyer also listened to Marjorie Fair to help her write Bella's emotions in *New Moon*. "It's just heartbreaking music where the pain is done so beautifully," Meyer told *Entertainment Weekly*. "It really got me in the zone for writing about a person who is horribly depressed and yet not at all showing it."

Songs by the band My Chemical Romance helped Meyer write romantic scenes. The music especially helped her get in touch with Jacob's character and with the feelings of vulnerably and of brashly falling in love for the first time. As Meyer said, the story is "not about some person who's grown up and [calloused] over and learned how to control things."

Channeling Jacob: Meyer used music by the band My Chemical Romance (*above*) to write scenes featuring Jacob in *New Moon*.

Meyer gives her mother, Candy, credit for helping her with the ending of *New Moon*. Meyer let Candy read what Meyer thought was the final draft of the manuscript. Candy suggested that the book needed more action at the end. Meyer wasn't sure. She was fairly attached to the ending as it stood. But maybe her mom was right, she thought. "I stewed about it and revised the ending," said Meyer.

First Book Published

Meyer was overjoyed when *Twilight* was released in October 2005. At first she fretted that the book might be a flop, but her worries proved unnecessary. By November the book was at the No. 5 spot on the *New York Times* best seller list for Children's Chapter Books. It also created a stir among readers, the news media, and book critics. People everywhere seemed to be talking about *Twilight*, and the "Mormon mom" from Phoenix who had made a splash on the literary scene.

First book: *Twilight* was an instant hit when released in October 2005.

Meyer traveled around the country and the world to promote *Twilight*. She appeared on television and gave newspaper and magazine interviews. When she made a bookstore appearance, crowds gathered to see her and hear her speak. Meyer noticed that more and more people showed up at her appearances each month. With the success of *Twilight*, Meyer was becoming famous. Her family helped to keep her grounded. "I think that after 30 years of being the most normal person in the whole world, it's really hard to become ungrounded," said Meyer of her newfound fame. "When I'm not out on tour or doing photo shoots, I tend to just forget about it all."

Meyer dedicated *Twilight* to her big sister, Emily. She acknowledged that the book might never have been completed without Emily's enthusiasm and encouragement.

Fans and Foes

Twilight received mixed reviews. "The novel's danger-factor skyrockets as the excitement of secret love and hushed affection morphs into a terrifying race to stay alive," said a reviewer in *School Library Journal*, a magazine that critiques children's and young adult literature. "Realistic, subtle, succinct, and easy to follow, *Twilight* will have readers dying to sink their teeth into it."

"Meyer has, like one of her vampires, turned into something rare and more than merely human: a literary phenomenon," said a reporter. *Publishers Weekly*, a U.S. book-publishing and bookselling magazine, voted *Twilight* the Best Book of the Year.

Many critics gave *Twilight* good reviews, but others ripped the book apart. "All plot and no style and not a lot of substance," wrote Jo De Guia in *The Bookseller*, a British trade magazine. She added, "There was nothing underneath the storyline at all; very little characterization and fairly poorly written. [It] had the potential to be so much more frightening and horrifying. But with so little left to the imagination and no connection with the main protagonist it left me cold."

Some reviewers remarked that *Twilight* had too much romance and not enough action. Laura Yao commented in the *Washington Post* that "discussions of feelings and emotions and such fill Meyer's [book]. Ick." She added, "Meyer lingers for pages at a time on [Edward and Bella's] exchanged looks, passionate declarations and innocent touches."

Messages in *Twilight*

Some people have questioned the messages that Meyer's vampire books are sending young women. Amy Clarke, an instructor in the University of California Davis writing program, teaches a popular course on

Character development: Some critics of *Twilight* do not like the way girls are portrayed in the books. But Meyer *(shown above)* said she writes things that entertain her.

the Harry Potter books. Compared to Harry Potter, Clarke said, *Twilight* is "much more of a girl's book." In an interview with the *Washington Post*, Clarke wondered if *Twilight* is sending a sexist message to young women. "Do we really want our daughters," she asked, "reading books about a girl like Bella who is always needing to be saved, who is willing to give up her mortality for a boy?"

Similarly, a few critics claimed that Meyer disregards women's rights and independence—even that she is antifeminist. Meyer strongly disagrees. She said, with her usual sense of humor, "If anything, I am antihuman."

Teacher Deborah Brady said she consumed the *Twilight* series "in one gulp." What interested her most about the books was the romantic tension that develops between Edward and Bella.

However, when Brady first started reading the series, she questioned the messages in *Twilight* and its sequels. As a schoolteacher, she wondered if the books might be sending young women harmful messages about relationships. "Initially, I was concerned that Edward was using the language of a potential abuser," said Brady. "He kept telling Bella that he was bad for her. There seemed to be a dangerous edge to him that did not put her off."

But as she read on, Brady's opinion of Edward and Bella's relationship changed. "Later, Edward seemed to be more of an old-fashioned gentleman," said Brady. "A guy who (at first) seems to be a little authoritarian and in control. Girl who asserts her power. Girl who wants to have sex. Guy putting on the brakes. Very interesting male-female dynamics!"[49]

Meyer says she doesn't write messages in her books. "I always write things that entertain me, and one of the things I find really enjoyable to explore is the idea of love," she says. "I like looking at my own life and my friends and family and how love changes who you are. It fascinates me."

If anything, Meyer says, her books are about choice. "I really think that's the underlying metaphor of my vampires." The Cullens are transformed into vampires, but they consciously decide to avoid taking human lives. "It doesn't matter where you're stuck in life," Meyer explains, "or what you think you have to do; you can always choose something else. There's always a different path."

New Moon: The Book Release

In September 2006, a little more than a year after *Twilight*'s publication, the first sequel, *New Moon*, was released. Fans of *Twilight* waited in long lines at bookstores around the country to claim their copies of *New Moon*. Like *Twilight*, *New Moon* grabbed the No. 5 position on the *New York Times* best seller list within days. In the book's second week, it jumped to the No. 1 position, where it remained for more than thirty weeks.

New Moon: The second book in Meyer's *Twilight* series was released in September 2006.

As Meyer toured bookstores to promote *New Moon*, fans met her with the same zeal with which they read her books. Megan Tingley of Little, Brown attended one of Meyer's Barnes & Noble (a U.S. bookstore chain) appearances to celebrate the new release. "The kids had been cutting school to get these tickets and waiting in line forever," recalled Tingley. "When Meyer came out, these girls next to me started trembling and crying and grabbing each other. It was crazy." Tingley compared the experience to the screaming crowds that greeted rock musicians and singers in the 1950s and 1960s. It was, she said, like watching "the newsreels of the Beatles or Elvis [Presley]."

Despite being adored by her fans, negative reviews of her books bother Meyer. "It's a bit hard for me: I'm very thin-skinned. I used to read all the reviews on Amazon.com," she said. "I could read 100 five-star glowing reviews and the one review that's one-star—'This is trash'—that's the one that sticks with me."

Eclipsed by Harry Potter?

In summer 2007, Meyer's third book in the *Twilight* series, *Eclipse*, was nearing publication. But another big book loomed on the literary horizon. J. K. Rowling's much-anticipated *Harry Potter and the Deathly*

Book rivals: Kids line up to get their copy of *Harry Potter and the Deathly Hallows* in Tempe, Arizona, in July 2007. The book came out just one month before Meyer's *Eclipse*.

Hallows was due to arrive in bookstores just days before *Eclipse*. Meyer was worried. She knew how popular the Harry Potter books were. She herself was a big fan of J. K. Rowling. Meyer called her publisher and "pitched a huge fit because I did not want my book to come out so close to hers. I saw a tidal wave of *Harry Potter* that would erase *Eclipse*. They said 'trust us,'" recalled Meyer."

Meyer's publisher was correct. *Eclipse* was released on August 7, 2007. Nearly 150,000 copies sold in the first twenty-four hours of its

Phenomenon: *Eclipse,* the third installment in Meyer's series, was released in August 2007.

debut. By the end of the next year, the novel had sold more than 4.5 million copies.

Once again, Meyer hit the road to promote the new book. At a book signing for *Eclipse* in Vermont, a fan asked Meyer which character from the *Twilight* series she relates to most. "Well, in so far as feeling vulnerably human and female, Bella," said Meyer. "But then, the way I look at the world is a lot closer to Edward's vision of things." Meyer added, "And then I have my Jacob moments, too, when I'm, like, 'whatever.'" The crowd—many of them apparently Jacob fans—screamed loudly.

Something new: Meyer released *The Host*, a science fiction novel for adults, in May 2008. Here Meyer holds a copy at a book signing in California.

Prolific Author

In May 2008, Meyer surprised her fans by writing outside the vampire genre. She released a science fiction novel, *The Host*. It was also her first book written intentionally for an adult audience. Meyer felt pleased with her new book. She wanted to be known as more than a writer of vampire stories. *The Host* debuted in the No. 1 spot on both the *New York Times* and the *Wall Street Journal* best seller lists.

The idea for *The Host* came to Meyer before she began writing the fourth *Twilight* book, *Breaking Dawn*. She had been talking to a friend about "the idea of not having a body, just an idea of someone who could have two personalities in the same body and they're both in love with the same person and how that would work." Meyer's idea grew, and before she knew it, she had written a full-length, science fiction novel set in the distant future on Earth.

In the story, an alien named Wanderer is melded with a dying woman named Melanie. Together in one body, the two women try to find the last surviving people on the planet. They also fall in love with the same man.

Meyer wanted to promote her books, but when she was on the road, she missed her kids and husband terribly. Pancho decided to quit his job as an accountant in 2008. Though the family had hired a nanny to help out, he wanted to spend more time with the kids when

Out and about: Meyer toured to promote *The Host* in the United States and overseas. Here she poses next to a promotional poster at a book signing at the Mall of America in Bloomington, Minnesota.

Meyer was on the road. He also took on the full-time task of managing Meyer's growing finances. As a professional accountant, Pancho was well-suited to the job.

In June 2008, Meyer stopped in Berlin, Germany, on her book tour for *The Host*. She told fans that she was working on a sequel to the novel and it was almost done. And she said that she had another sequel to *The Host* mapped out in her head. Meyer's energy and imagination appeared to be unstoppable.

Meyer traveled, made bookstore appearances, and gave press interviews to promote *The Host*. All the while, she worked on a sequel to the book and other writing projects. In July, Meyer told the press that she had written four chapters of a ghost story called "Summer House," and a "time-travel novel that she figured out the ending to . . . while putting on her make-up."

Meyer finally returned home to Arizona, exhausted. But her work was far from done. Her editor informed her that she had just three days to put the finishing touches on *Breaking Dawn*. Meyer worked eighteen-hour days to complete the project. Because of the stress she was under, Meyer jokingly referred to the project as "Breaking Down."

"The last 12 months seem like 10 years," Meyer told *People Weekly* in 2008. "My mom worries, 'Are you getting enough rest?'"

USA TODAY Snapshots®

More fiction-reading a fact

Percentage who read fiction[1]:

45% — 2002

47% — 2008

1 – Novel or short story
Source: National Endowment for the Arts, Reading on the Rise, 2009

By Michelle Healy and Sam Ward, USA TODAY, 2009

On tour: Meyer *(right)* toured with musician Justin Furstenfeld *(left)*, of the band Blue October, to promote the release of *Breaking Dawn*.

"Delicious Cheesecake"

In July 2008, Stephenie Meyer fans excitedly awaited the release of her fourth *Twilight* installment. Meyer appeared in four major cities to promote *Breaking Dawn*. Musician Justin Furstenfeld, front man for the band Blue October, appeared as Meyer's opening act. Fans tried to guess how Meyer would wrap up the *Twilight* saga. Would Bella end up with Edward? With Jacob? Or would there be a big surprise ending? At one bookstore event, an eleven-year-old fan asked Meyer about her upcoming release. "Are we going to feel complete at the end of *Breaking Dawn*?" asked the girl. "I can't really answer that question for you," Meyer responded. "But I felt closure."

"There's no way to please everybody," said Meyer, about the much-discussed series conclusion. "The [e-mail] messages I get say, 'If Bella doesn't end up with Edward forever, I'm going to burn this book,' and the next one I get will say, 'If Bella doesn't end up with Jacob forever, I'll burn this book,'" said Meyer. "So that's a problem, but this is the ending I wanted all along. That's the important thing. I think people will be happy, though."

Patriots at

USA

nearly catches swift

Brady: To g

Goog

xus On e-whiz

dnesday,

Ne

IN F**O**CUS

Meyer's Favorite Character?

Fans often ask Meyer who she likes best in her *Twilight* series. "Okay, who's my favorite character? And then after that, can I tell you who my favorite child is?" Meyer said, joking with a fan at a San Francisco, California, book signing. She explained that she couldn't answer the question because she loves "everybody in different ways and at different times."

One fan asked her if the character, Edward, was based on someone she knew. Many of Meyer's *Twilight* characters—such as Mike, Jessica, Lauren, and Eric—are composites of people she had known in high school. Edward, on the other hand, had appeared in a dream. He was unlike anyone she had ever known.

When Meyer was writing a scene that had both Edward and Jacob in it, Meyer's job as a writer was especially exciting. "I just cannot look away from the [computer] screen when I'm doing that," said Meyer. "So when those two are together, it just takes on a life of its own."

Some of Meyer's characters amuse her more than others. "I mean the people that make me laugh when

Alice and Jacob: Actors Ashley Greene *(left)* and Taylor Lautner play the characters Alice and Jacob in the *Twilight* movies.

I'm writing are Alice and Jacob," says Meyer. "They're always—again, I'm sounding crazy—they say things that surprise me and that's fun."

Pet projects drop by about a third

9,297 'earmarks' for 2010 spending bills cost $10.2B

By Matt Kelley
USA TODAY

WASHINGTON — The 2010 federal spending bills disclose $10.2 billion for pet projects inserted by members of Congress, a drop of nearly a third since

Another Meyer fan asked her if Edward would stop loving Bella if she became a vampire. Would he no longer be drawn to her human blood? "You have to look at it this way," said Meyer. "To Edward, Bella is like a delicious cheesecake—and no one can resist a delicious cheesecake. It's why he noticed her the first time. But he truly loves her the way she is. It's not about the smell, because it's like they are soulmates."

Readers asked Meyer if she was completely done with the *Twilight* series. Meyer explained that *Breaking Dawn* would be the last book in the series told from the perspective of Bella. "We'll see. It's all about the time. *Midnight Sun* [a work-in-progress that

For the fans: Meyer answered fans' questions at events in four cities to promote the release of *Breaking Dawn*. Here she speaks to an audience in New York City in August 2008.

tells the *Twilight* story from Edward's perspective] needs to be done as well. I have so many ideas, but I want to write other stories, too."

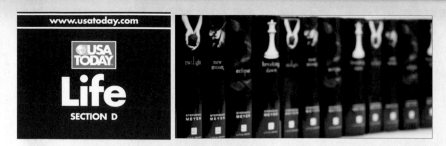

July 31, 2008

Meyer unfazed as fame dawns

<u>From the Pages of</u>
<u>USA TODAY</u>

Stephenie Meyer is the most famous writer you've never heard of.

But not for long. Meyer's growing popularity is like a flashing billboard on our pop culture landscape.

The 34-year-old creator of the *Twilight* teen vampire series is so sizzling hot, it's not a stretch to suggest she's heir apparent to J.K. Rowling, who gave the world Harry Potter.

The self-assured Meyer doesn't seem rattled by the comparison.

"There will never be another J.K. Rowling. That's a lot of pressure on me, isn't it?" says Meyer, curled up on a leather sofa in her comfortable and airy adobe-style home in this sun-scorched desert community north of Phoenix. "I'm just happy being Stephenie Meyer. That's cool enough for me."

Meyer may be cool and composed, but her ravenous fans are in a frenzy. They've devoured the first three Twilight saga novels and are ready to pounce when *Breaking Dawn*, the fourth and final book, goes on sale Saturday at 12:01 A.M. amid midnight-party madness.

And they're already overheated about *Twilight* the movie, which doesn't hit theaters until Dec. 12.

What's all the fuss about?

It starts with an otherwordly love triangle: human teenager Bella Swan, her hunky vampire boyfriend Edward Cullen and Jacob Black, the irascible [hot-tempered] werewolf who also loves her. Fans are waiting to find out who Bella chooses, and if her choice means that she, too, will become a vampire.

The numbers tell the story:

- After three years, nearly 8 million copies of Meyer's first three books in print in the USA; *Twilight*, the first in the series, was published in 2005.
- The first printing of *Breaking Dawn* is 3.2 million, the highest yet for a Meyer book.
- Meyer has dominated USA TODAY's Best-Selling Books list this summer. *Twilight* is No. 1 this week; the second and third books, *New Moon* (2006) and *Eclipse*

(2007) are Nos. 2 and 4. Her first adult novel, *The Host*, a story of aliens published in May with 930,000 in print, is No. 15.

Booksellers are turning *Breaking Dawn*'s release into an event. More than 1,500 bookstores will stay open late Friday to host parties, contests and games.

Meyer is limiting her appearances to a handful of venues that can handle thousands of fans—if they were lucky to snag a ticket. Events in New York and Los Angeles sold out in 45 minutes. "Fans just can't wait to find out what happens in the last book," says Diane Mangan of Borders [a bookstore chain].

Who personifies the typical fan is surprising. Little, Brown publishes the series under its Books for Young Readers division, but many adults are fans.

On top of the world: Meyer poses holding *Breaking Dawn*, her fifth book to be on the best seller lists.

"I was instantly hooked," says Lisa Hansen, 35, of Utah County, Utah, a married mother of children ages 5 and 9. She discovered the series last summer, then created twilightmoms.com, a fan site where thousands of adults discuss the books.

"I feel an emotional connection with the characters," says Hansen. "It's almost like a realistic relationship that you would have with somebody."

For younger readers, the appeal is "the combination of the love story, the action and the danger," says Marie Southard, 17, of Forked River, N.J., who was obsessed with Potter before she became hooked on *Twilight*.

Meyer says she owes a lot to her fans, but when the hoopla surrounding *Breaking Dawn* and *Twilight* the movie settles down, she's looking forward to doing what she loves best—writing more books.

"I'm just going to try and stay home and write five books next year," Meyer says. "It may not happen, but that's my goal. And I'm not going to let anyone see them. It's just going to be about sitting home and writing."

—Carol Memmott

Breaking Dawn Breaks Out

On August 2, 2008, four thousand bookstores around the United States held parties to celebrate the release of *Breaking Dawn*. Fans showed up dressed in *Twilight*-themed costumes. Readers were eager to know what was going to happen to their favorite characters. Many fans started reading the book as soon as they bought it, standing or sitting in the bookstore.

Breaking Dawn sold 1.3 million copies on its first day of release. *Breaking Dawn* immediately seized the No. 1 position on best seller lists around the world.

Big sales: Customers buy *Breaking Dawn* at a bookstore party in New York City on the day of its release.

Phenomenon: Stephenie poses with a poster for *Breaking Dawn* during one of her appearances to promote the book in August 2008.

At a bookstore release for *Breaking Dawn* in New York City, Meyer received "rock star treatment from fans," according to *People Weekly*. Meyer appeared at a few carefully selected venues that could handle crowds of hundreds of people.

Fan Alesha Lurie said she stayed up until three in the morning to finish the fourth book in the series. "I had to know what was going to happen," she said. She wasn't disappointed in how Meyer concluded the saga. "The fourth book was my favorite. Everything worked out the way I thought it should work out."

"The series got better and better," added Lurie. "All of the books were just as good. You don't want to go anywhere. You can't do anything but read the dang book!"

CHAPTER SIX

Movie madness: Fans line up for the premiere of *Twilight* in Los Angeles, California, in November 2008.

Twilight Premieres

In the fall of 2008, movie studio Summit Entertainment released the much-anticipated film version of *Twilight* in theaters worldwide.

When Meyer sold rights to the company to produce her film, she had put a special rule in the contract. Referring to LDS Church rules on movie ratings, Meyer said, "I put in a clause ... that the movie had to be PG-13 [not R rated] so I could go see it."

Film critic Richard Corliss, writing in *Time* magazine, compared the love story in *Twilight* to that of classic films *Rebel Without a Cause*, *West Side Story*, and *Romeo and Juliet*. "Bella could be any Hollywood heroine in love with a good boy whom society callously misunderstands," said Corliss. He noted that while the film "isn't a masterpiece," it "rekindles the warmth of great Hollywood romances."

The sound track for *Twilight* featured some of Meyer's favorite bands, including Muse, Linkin Park, and Paramore. And Meyer appears briefly in the film, playing herself. In an early scene, Bella Swan and her father are having dinner in the local diner. Meyer is seated at the diner's counter in front of a laptop computer. The waitress brings her a veggie plate (Meyer is a vegetarian in real life) and refers to Meyer by name.

Meyer didn't care for her on-screen debut. She "felt really awkward," and she covers her eyes every time she watches the scene. Meyer did, however, enjoy visiting the movie set and being a part of

On set: Meyer *(right)* enjoyed visiting the set of the *Twilight* production. She is shown here with director Catherine Hardwicke *(left)* and Kristen Stewart *(center)*, who plays Bella.

the filming. "I love watching the actors make dozens of minute shifts for each take of a scene, so that the director has a variety to work with when he starts cutting it together. I love it when everything comes together just right, and even on the tiny monitor, with no music and no editing, you can see that something exceptional just happened. It's a cool process, and one I never expected to have the opportunity to be involved with."

Meyer thought actor Kristen Stewart was a great fit for the role of Bella. She also thought that Robert Pattinson "nailed" the character of the vampire Edward. "He's not playing a version of Edward, he's playing Edward," said Meyer. In terms of physical appearance, "there is still quite a difference between Rob's Edward and the Edward in my head, but there are moments when they look eerily similar," said Meyer. "I'm still not sure how he does it, but I'm glad he can."

Casting: Meyer thought Robert Pattinson as Edward and Kristen Stewart as Bella were good choices for the *Twilight* movie adaptation. In this scene, Edward and Bella dance at their prom.

"A Movie Can't Be Like a Book"

Both fans and movie critics debated whether the actors in the movie matched the vision they had of the characters, in their minds, when they read the book.

"The book describes Edward as being jaw dropping, knock dead gorgeous; that any room he walks into every girl is in awe," said a female reader in her thirties, who didn't think Pattinson was a good fit for the role of Edward. "I don't think Robert Pattinson is gorgeous in that way. I think he is nice looking but that's it."

Two writers: Meyer *(left)* poses with Melissa Rosenberg at the *Twilight* movie premiere. Rosenberg is the screenwriter for the *Twilight* saga movies. She turns Meyer's books into screenplays that are used to shoot the films.

"He's a good Edward," said fan Alesha Lurie. "But I wish they'd put more steam—more passion—on the movie screen. I wanted more of how they [Edward and Bella] can't live without each other. But, overall, they did a good job. A movie can't be like a book."

A Girl Thing?

"In my experience, very few boys check out Meyer's books," says school librarian Ann Shubert. "I think the books are a girl and woman phenomenon. Because it is girl identified, any boy who likes it would not likely admit it. I do remember one eighth-grade boy who checked out a copy of Meyer's *New Moon*—supposedly for his sister."

In countries outside the United States, Meyer's male and female fans may be less divided. Martin Romero is a fifteen-year-old from Mexico. He read the *Twilight* books in Spanish after seeing the movie with his sister. "I was enchanted by the love that Edward and Bella felt for each other," said Martin.

In January 2009, *USA Today* announced that Stephenie Meyer had grabbed the top four spots on the newspaper's Top 100 Books of 2008. *Twilight* stood at No. 1, followed by *New Moon*, *Breaking Dawn*, and *Eclipse*. No other author had ever occupied the top four spots on the list. *USA Today* also named Meyer its Author of the Year.

After discovering the series, Martin recommended the books to his friends, both male and female. Martin and his friends created a *Twilight* fan site. They also formed a fan club at his school. They made *Twilight* T-shirts, handing them out to more than fifty classmates. When asked what he thought about *Twilight* having more female fans than male fans, Martin responded, "I think that *Twilight* is cool for guys."

The New J. K. Rowling?

Many people have compared Stephenie Meyer to J. K. Rowling. Meyer and Rowling have several things in common. Like Meyer, Rowling's Harry Potter manuscript received many rejections (twelve for Rowling, fourteen for Meyer) before being accepted by a publisher. Rowling's Harry Potter books, like Meyer's *Twilight* series, have created

Fan favorite: *Twilight* fans all over the world attend events and dress up like their favorite characters. This fan dressed up like one of the Volturi vampires at an event in 2009 in Volterra, Italy.

detailed fantasy worlds to draw in readers. Fans dress up like the characters. They wait in long lines at bookstores to grab their first copy of a new release. And like the Harry Potter books, Meyer's best sellers have been made into blockbuster movies.

Writer Lev Grossman compared the two authors in *Time* magazine. "Both writers embed their fantasy in the modern world," said Grossman. "Meyer's vampires are [as] contemporary as Rowling's wizards." And like Rowling's fans, Meyer's fans "do not want to just read [her] books; they want to climb inside them and live there."

Meyer credits Rowling for turning kids on to long books. Before Rowling, says Meyer, "People wouldn't put an 800-page YA book on the shelf because there was no way kids were going to read it. Now everyone knows that kids love big books. You just have to make them interesting for them."

Jan D., a youth librarian in Minnesota, isn't a *Twilight* fan. Though she herself hasn't read the books, she says, "My teen readers at the library—the ones who read voraciously and were reading before *Twilight* came along—tell me [the *Twilight* books are] not all that well-written. J. K. Rowling set the standard for making reading fun, and she did it for both boys and girls. I've read all the Harry Potter books, and I couldn't even begin to crack open *Twilight*."

Some Rowling fans don't read Meyer's books and vice versa. But many of Meyer's fans are J. K. Rowling fans as well. "I read Harry Potter three times—I liked it so well," said Alesha Lurie. "But I like Stephenie Meyer better than J. K. Rowling. Rowling's books were well written and easy to read, but they didn't grab my emotions like Stephenie Meyer's books did."

> In 2008 *Twilight* the movie earned $382 million in theaters worldwide. It earned an additional $157 million in DVD sales in North America.

Other popular authors also have their opinions about Meyer compared to Rowling. Stephen King, who penned his own vampire story in 1975, *Salem's Lot*, isn't a fan of Meyer's writing. In 2009 King spoke to a *USA Weekend* reporter and compared the writing of Meyer and Rowling. Both writers are "speaking directly to young people," said King, "The real difference is that Jo Rowling is a terrific writer and Stephenie Meyer can't write worth a darn. She's not very good."

Meyer's devout fans took insult at the horror writer's comments, their rage spilling over Internet fan pages. "King is no Gabriel Garcia Marquez [a Nobel Prize winning novelist]," commented a reader, "so I don't understand why he gets to say who is a good writer and who is not."

www.usatoday.com

USA TODAY

Life

SECTION D

November 6, 2009

It's 'Twilight' time in the Pacific Northwest

From the Pages of USA TODAY

Tiny Forks, Wash., (pop. 3,192) has seen visitation jump 600% since Stephenie Meyer's first teen-vampire novel was released in 2005, says Marcia Bingham, director of the Forks Chamber of Commerce.

"We're reveling in it," Bingham says of the fan attention. "And they don't complain about the rain!"

Here are some places where you can sink your teeth into *Twilight*:

- Forks, Wash. This logging town on the Olympic Peninsula is considered Vampire Central. A free map outlines *Twilight* touchstones such as Forks Community Hospital and Forks High School. Tours are conducted by Dazzled by Twilight.
- La Push, Wash. Home of the Quileute tribe, La Push boasts werewolf-friendly First Beach—an essential stop for aficionados of [those who like] *Twilight*'s Jacob. Native American-owned Occanside Resort is offering packages and specials, including one that includes firewood for your own beach bonfire.
- Portland, Ore., area. Producers shot much of *Twilight* in St. Helens, near the Columbia River Gorge. (Bella's house is here, as is the Italian restaurant where Edward and Bella have their first date.) Events are planned around the *New Moon* opening weekend. In nearby Corbett, the View Point Inn—site of the prom scene—offers a *Twilight* slumber party package, a reservation-only *Twilight* menu and tours.
- Vancouver, British Columbia. Fans searching for RPazz (as star Robert Pattinson has been dubbed) have been hanging out north of the border, shooting site for *New Moon* and for *Eclipse*, the third series installment set for release in June 2010.

—Chris Gray Faust

Robert Pattinson

The Twilight Tour

Stephenie Meyer has made the real Forks, Washington, famous. About 15 miles (24 kilometers) from the Pacific coast, the small town has become the destination for serious *Twilight* fans.

Hannah Howard, eighteen, of Eugene, Oregon, drove seven hours to tour Forks with her sister and a friend. "We stayed at a *Twilight*-themed hotel, where everything from the bedspreads to the wall paper was all Twilighted out. We went to Forks High school, the hospital where we saw Dr. Cullen's parking space. . . . We went to the police station, where there was a huge shrine of *Twilight* memorabilia."[96] (Bella's father, Charlie Swan, is Forks's fictional police chief.)

While in Forks, Howard met *Twilight* fans from all over the world, including Japan and Switzerland. "It was amazing," she said, "being surrounded by other die-hard fans like myself."

In Forks, *Twilight* fans can order Bellasagna, EdBread, or a Swan Salad at Pacific Pizza. Forks Coffee Shop offers Jacob's Blackberry Cobbler. Sully's Drive-In grills Bella Burgers, with a choice of vegetarian or meat patties. "[Fans] love to take pictures by our sign, and they just keep coming," said Bruce Guckenberg, Sully's owner.

In *Twilight*, Bella and Edward have their first date at the Bella Italia restaurant in Port Angeles. Bella orders mushroom lasagna. As a result, the real-life eatery added mushroom pasta to the menu. Meyer eats at Bella Italia when in town. Meyer, said Bella Italia's owner, Neil Conklin, "is really down-to-earth and good natured."

Take a tour: Visitors to Forks, Washington, can take guided *Twilight* tours on this bus and view this replica of Bella's 1953 truck *(right)*.

"A Need to Read"

Many of Meyer's fans are moved by the strength of her storytelling and her talent for taking a reader inside a story. "When I started reading the *Twilight* series, I was hooked," said a teenaged reader. "I had never experienced a need to read like I did when I opened the first book. Anyone who can capture my attention like she did, in my opinion, is a great writer."

Best-selling writer Jodi Picoult agrees. Picoult is the author of young adult novels such as *My Sister's Keeper* and *Second Glance*. She credits Meyer for inspiring kids to read. She acknowledges that some of her readers come to her because of the *Twilight* series. "Stephenie Meyer has gotten people hooked on books," says Picoult, "and that's good for all of us."

Author support: Best-selling author Jodi Picoult *(above)* has defended Meyer to critics. She says that Meyer gets people hooked on reading.

Book club: A language arts teacher in California asks a trivia question about *Twilight* at a book club the school hosts for students.

"We've had many, many teen girls in asking for books like *Twilight*," said a youth librarian. "That's a perfect gateway to sharing with them all kinds of other books, from vampire stories to love stories to high-tension action stories."

"Many teens want to connect with their peers, so if 'everyone' is reading a book, they'll read it, too," said another children's librarian. She added, "And whether the books are written well (or not), they tell a story well and have a lot the teens can identify with and appreciate."

Some librarians and parents find the material in Meyer's books inappropriate for very young readers. Meyer herself feels that *Twilight* and its sequels aren't appropriate for young children. She thinks that teens aged fifteen and up are better suited to handle the material in her books.

Despite the criticism, Meyer's fans are steadfast and believe in her writing abilities. "Any author that can touch a reader's feelings so passionately is amazing," said Christine, a teacher from the Pacific Northwest.

The Price of Fame

Meyer was thrilled about the success of her books. But, at the same time, she was also learning about the high price of fame. She became a celebrity known by millions of people around the world, and a few of those people were trying to take advantage of her star status.

For example, while working on the manuscript of *Midnight Sun*, Meyer entrusted a copy to a friend. The manuscript found its way into the wrong hands, and someone posted the incomplete book on the Internet. Many readers, eager to read the book, downloaded illegal copies of the manuscript. Meyer was devastated by the event. She made a lengthy statement about the incident on her official website.

"I did not want my readers to experience *Midnight Sun* before it was completed, edited and published," Meyer wrote on her website. "I think it is important for everybody to understand that what happened was a huge violation of my rights as an author, not to mention me as a human being." She continued, "In any case, I feel too sad about what has happened to continue working on *Midnight Sun*, and so it is on hold indefinitely."

Meyer considered the leaked draft of her manuscript "messy and flawed and full of mistakes." Nonetheless, after the incident, she posted a partial draft of *Midnight Sun* on her website. She wanted her fans to be able to sample the yet-unreleased book without feeling guilty for downloading an illegal copy off the Internet.

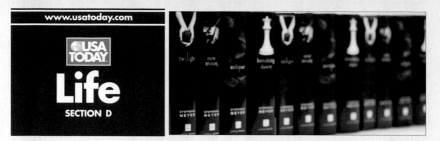

July 16, 2009

Harlequin aims to court young-adult readers

From the Pages of
<u>USA TODAY</u>

Harlequin is feeling like a kid again.

The 60-year-old publisher of classic bodice-rippers [historical romance novels] is rolling out its newest imprint: Harlequin Teen.

"These books specifically focus on teen protagonists [main characters], which is not something Harlequin has done a whole lot of," says the publisher's Natashya Wilson.

Add Harlequin to the list of publishers that have fallen hard for teen readers, thanks to the seismic sales of Stephenie Meyer's teen vampire series *Twilight*.

"These will be titles specifically developed for readers of *Twilight*," says Wilson, as well as fans of other popular young-adult authors including Sarah Dessen (*Along for the Ride*) and Elizabeth Scott (*Living Dead Girl*).

Other publishers—including HarperTeen and Razorbill—are already benefiting from the growing hunger for teen romances laced with supernatural and paranormal elements.

So far, almost 20 [Harlequin Teen] titles are planned for 2010. They will be a mix of paranormal, science fiction and contemporary romance.

Romance, according to Business of Consumer Book Publishing, an industry report, is the biggest fiction category in the USA, with more than 8,000 titles published in 2008. Paranormal romances make up a huge portion.

Harlequin's move is a smart one, says Kathleen Adey of Romance Writers of America.

"The teen-romance readers of today are the adult-romance readers of tomorrow. Courting them when they are younger is probably a good thing."

—Carol Memmott

"Fun While It Lasted"

In June 2009, Meyer discovered that impostors, pretending to be her, were popping up on the Internet. As a result, she decided to shut down both her MySpace and Twitter social networking accounts. "It was a lot of fun while it lasted, and I really miss the early days when I could hang out with people online," said Meyer. "I wish it was easier for me to talk to everyone the way I used to."

Meyer had enjoyed "tweeting" with her readers on Twitter.com. And it had been fun having more than twenty-five thousand MySpace friends. But Meyer didn't want her fans to confuse her real words with the postings of impostors. She decided to close her accounts on the popular websites. Meyer warned her fans, "If you're communicating with someone online who you think is me, it's not."

USA TODAY Snapshots®

The nation's best sellers

Top five best sellers, shown in proportion of sales. Example: For every 10 copies of Glenn Beck's *Common Sense* sold, 8.4 copies of *Harry Potter and the Deathly Hallows* were sold:

Glenn Beck's Common Sense Glenn Beck	10
Harry Potter and the Deathly Hallows J.K. Rowling	8.4
New Moon Stephenie Meyer	7.2
Eclipse Stephenie Meyer	6.2
My Sister's Keeper Jodi Picoult	6.2

Thursday: Top 50 books list (top150.usatoday.com)

Source: USA TODAY Best-Selling Books   USA TODAY, 2009

Meyer receives hundreds of letters from fans each week. It's hard for her to know that stacks and stacks of letters are sitting unanswered. She can't possibly read, much less answer, all of them. "It's a huge source of guilt," says Meyer. "If I could stop time, I would sit down and write everyone a three-page letter. There's just no physical way for me to do that, so I feel awful."

New Moon: Meyer signs autographs for fans lined up outside the premiere of *The Twilight Saga: New Moon* on November 16, 2009, in California.

Bright Future

On Friday, November 20, 2009, *The Twilight Saga: New Moon* opened in theaters worldwide. The *Twilight* sequel on the big screen earned $72.7 million on its first day. *New Moon* broke a new record for making more money on its opening day than any film in history. *New Moon*'s one-day record totaled $3 million more than *Twilight* earned for the entire premiere weekend.

The film received mixed reviews and feedback from fans. "I liked *New Moon* even better than the *Twilight* movie," said a fan. "I thought

[*New Moon*] stuck with the book better than the first movie."

Many reviewers didn't agree. "One moody high school girl lusts after an even moodier vampire and the result is a potential $100 million opening weekend at the box office? . . . Make. It. Stop. Seriously," complained reporter Mara Reinstein on the *Huffington Post* website. "What was an amusing little fervor last year has spiraled into an out-of-control phenomenon."

Some critics poked fun at actors in the film. "As Edward, Pattinson is all pale passion and tortured restraint; his eyebrows, like muskrats determined to mate, hunch together in the middle of his sunken face; the few times he smiles, it looks as if it hurts," said Nancy Gibbs, a writer for *Time* magazine.

Second movie: *(Left to right)* Robert Pattinson, director Chris Weitz, Kristen Stewart, and Taylor Lautner promote *New Moon* in Spain in 2009.

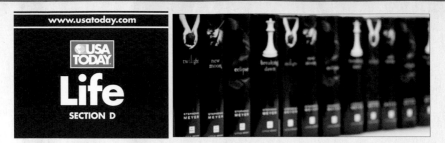
November 6, 2009

'New Moon'

From the Pages of
USA TODAY

On a college break, American teenager Kiersten Kunke and her friend, Canadian Stephanie Regier, plot their version of an Italian Grand Tour. On their must-see list: Florence, Venice, Rome—and Volterra?

This small Tuscan [part of a region in central Italy] city with an ancient history has become a cult destination among traveling teen-agers and people in their 20s (not to mention some vampire-loving mothers), thanks to the phenom-enon *Twilight*. In the series' second book, author Stephenie Meyer set a crucial scene between heroine Bella and her undead soul mate Edward in Volterra—and, as *The Twilight Saga: New Moon* prepares to open as a movie Nov. 20, fans are dying to retrace the tormented couple's steps.

Volterra: In *New Moon*, the Volturi—a coven of elite vampires—live in the clock tower on the Piazza dei Priori, the town square.

Volterra is capitalizing on the interest. The tourism office has created a themed map of the city, encouraged fan meet-ups, and this spring introduced a *New Moon* weekend package that includes a walking tour called "Hot on the Trail of Edward and Bella," *Twilight* merchandise and even a dramatic re-enactment of one of the book's scenes.

Volterra officials lobbied to have *New Moon* filmed there. But the film producers picked Montepulciano, another walled Tuscan town about 70 miles [113 km] south-east of Volterra, for the five-day shoot in May.

The *New Moon* shoot elevated Montepulciano from guidebooks to tabloids as media descended upon the town, hoping for candids of the young cast, particularly [actor Robert] Pattinson and his co-star Kristen Stewart.

—Chris Gray Faust

Moms and kids: A crowd of fans cheer during a 2009 DVD release party for the *Twilight* movie. "Team Edward" shirts and "Team Jacob" shirts are popular with fans of the books and movies.

Team Edward vs. Team Jacob

Since the dawn of *Twilight*, readers of the popular series have been divided about Bella Swan's two main love interests, Edward Cullen and Jacob Black. Fans wearing "Team Edward" or "Team Jacob" shirts show up at book signings and other *Twilight* events. Fans debate on Twitter about who is better for Bella, the vampire Edward or the werewolf Jacob. Stephenie Meyer's fans talk about the *Twilight* saga characters as if they are real people.

The movie premiere of *New Moon* intensified the debate. As in the book version, the character Edward is absent through much of the film. Viewers got to see much more of Bella's childhood friend and love interest, Jacob. Actor Taylor Lautner plays the teen werewolf.

Christine, the teacher from the Pacific Northwest, discussed her experience on the online social networking website Facebook after seeing the premiere of *New Moon*. "People [on Facebook] are saying that they are turning to Team Jacob and not Team Edward so much," she said.

November 23, 2009

Women mooning over teen 'Twilight'

From the Pages of USA TODAY It has been three days since *The Twilight Saga: New Moon* opened, and it's increasingly obvious that adult—even mature—women are making as much noise as teen girls over this tale of a great love between a teenage girl and a vampire, with a few werewolf complications.

Jenny West, 32, a New Jersey finance executive, set her boyfriend's eyes rolling with the life-size cardboard cutout of heartthrob vamp Edward Cullen (Robert Pattinson) in her dining room.

"There's no shame in loving a book about struggling vampires," West says.

No shame, indeed, not when there's so much money to be made. *New Moon* took in $140.7 million this weekend, according to studio estimates from Nielsen EDI.

It's moms and grandmas standing in line at theaters, reading and rereading the books, spending big bucks on the merchandise (such as Nordstrom's *Twilight*-themed apparel and jewelry) and writing reams of fan fiction (17,000 stories on just one fan-fiction site alone). They follow scores of blogs and websites, such as TwilightMoms.com, aimed at bringing together other adult fans all over the world.

For some, the sex appeal of Lautner's character in the sequel was a large part of the reason for changing loyalty. In one scene, Jacob comes to Bella's rescue after a motorcycle accident. He takes off his T-shirt to help nurse Bella's wound. "From that point on, his torso remains so central a character it should be given its own credit line," said *Time* critic Gibbs.

Fans of all ages: Fans stand in line with signs trying to catch the attention of stars of the *Twilight* movies.

"The appeal to a lot of us who are not teenagers is the community (of fellow fans) we've founded," West says. "It has really bloomed and become huge because we feed off each other."

Teens identify with Bella in fantasizing about their first love, says Lori Joffs , 35, a stay-at-home mom in Nashville [Tennessee]. "But as an adult who has faced reality, it's escapism of a different kind, remembering those first twitches of falling in love and reliving it through Bella."

—Maria Puente

Christine agrees. "When Jacob takes off his shirt in [*New Moon*]," she said, "every woman gasped and made some kind of noise. When Edward took his shirt off, nothing happened." She noted, "[Edward had] no sex appeal for me. Not like Jacob." After seeing the movie, Christine found herself joining Team Jacob. "It's funny, because when I read the book I was rooting for Edward the whole time," she explained.

Team Jacob: Actors Taylor Lautner *(left)* and Kristen Stewart act out a scene as Jacob and Bella in *The Twilight Saga: New Moon*. The character of Jacob has a bigger role in the second book in the *Twilight* series.

"When I watched the second movie, I wanted Jacob to win."

One fan asked Meyer what she thought of Lautner's portrayal of Jacob. "He's wonderful as the sweet kid, but even better as the angry werewolf," said Meyer. "The kid can act."

The trustworthy, likable Jacob is a Quileute Native American. Some fans appreciated the Native American themes in the story. "I liked how Stephenie Meyer put the Quileute culture into the story, especially the part about respecting the elders," said a reader. "You don't see that a lot in books. There isn't a lot—but it's there. People don't write about that stuff anymore."

Public Figure

Meyer's phenomenal rise to fame has changed her life in many ways. For example, she had to hire a bodyguard for protection when she makes public appearances. Security guards also protect her home.

Meyer finds it a bit challenging to balance being a celebrity writer with all the other roles in her life—mother, wife, daughter, and sister. The solitary work of writing comes easily to her. But she has also learned that she must be able to be "on" in public. "I have to be someone who can get up in front of 1,000 screaming people and talk," says Meyer. It does not come naturally, according to Meyer, who says she lacks confidence and doesn't think she is interesting.

Members of the press often ask Meyer personal questions, especially about her religion. They want to know why a devout Mormon is writing about vampires. "It seems funny that it's still a story," Meyer has said, "because you didn't hear people saying 'Jon Stewart, Jewish writer,' when his book came out. I guess being Mormon is just odd enough that people think it's still a real story. Obviously, to me, it seems super normal. It's just my religion."

Fans sometimes ask Meyer funny questions about her home life. A *Good Morning America* viewer once asked

Life of a writer: Meyer has had to learn how to balance time with her family, writing, and making public appearances to promote her books and the movies.

Meyer, "Does your husband ever get jealous of Edward?" Stephenie answered with a laugh: "No, he, he refuses to be jealous of fictional characters. He says, you know, 'I'm real, so I've got one on him there.'"

Happy Hermit

When Meyer isn't writing, traveling around the world to promote her books, attending film premieres, and being interviewed by countless members of the press, she likes to stay home. "I'm a hermit, basically," says Meyer. "I'm just that kind of person."

Meyer, Pancho, and their three children live in a modern, five-bedroom house, just outside of Phoenix in a town called Cave Creek. Giant saguaro cacti, native to the area, decorate the desert landscape. Meyer's parents and one of her brothers live in the neighborhood.

Home in the desert: Meyer, her husband, and children live in this house outside of Phoenix, Arizona. Behind the house is a pool and basketball and tennis courts.

"When I'm at home . . . I'm Mom," says Meyer. "Every day is kind of what you expect, very normal and standard, and then every now and then I have to be Stephenie Meyer and go on the road and have cameras pointed at me, but generally I get to just be me. It's cool."

Meyer's happiest when she's surrounded by her children, her husband, and her big extended family. The Meyers try to keep things as normal as possible for the kids. Pancho is a leader of his boys' Cub Scout troop. And the Meyers attend school band performances and Little League games.

When she can, Meyer just relaxes. For fun, she likes to see G-rated movies with her kids. She also enjoys lighthearted comedies, such as *Baby Mama*, with Tina Fey. "I love Tina Fey," says Meyer. "I think she may be the most adorable person on the face of the planet."

Meyer also enjoys watching TV. A favorite show is the crime drama *Law & Order*. "I can't move until it's over. If it's a marathon, the day's gone," Meyer told an interviewer from *Vogue*.

And she likes the cable channel Home and Garden Television (HGTV). HGTV features many programs about house hunting and home decorating. "I just love looking at all the houses and watching people get their houses all prettied up," says Meyer. "HGTV is a safe place, and everyone is always happy."

Meyer likes to shop for pretty clothes, red nail polish, and expensive shoes. One of her other favorite activities is sleeping. "I am addicted to sleep. That is my weakness, and so if I'm not getting eight hours, I'm not a happy person," says Meyer.

Dressed for success: Meyer likes to shop for clothes, such as the dress she wore to the premiere of *New Moon* in November 2009.

Sometimes Meyer and her family like to get away to their summer home, a Dutch-style farmhouse on Marrowstone Island in Washington State. Meyer and her husband purchased the $1.33 million waterfront property in the Pacific Northwest in 2007.

Working, spending time with family, and making the effort to unwind takes up much of Meyer's time. She finds that she doesn't read as much as she once did. However, she still reads Jane Austen's *Pride and Prejudice* at least once a year, just as she did as a girl. And her publisher

Vacation getaway: Meyer and her family have a summer home on Washington's Marrowstone Island. Pictured is the lighthouse on the island.

sends her advance copies of soon-to-be-released books. When she travels, she finds time to read when she's stuck in airports with nothing to do.

Writing On

Though Meyer has non-vampire writing projects in the works, the *Twilight* world she created continues to thrive. In 2009 Meyer announced that she was working on a graphic novel version of *Twilight* in partnership with Young Kim, a female Korean artist with a fine arts background.

Twilight Morphs to Merchandise

Meyer's *Twilight* books have morphed into a financial franchise of epic proportions—making the super-wealthy author even richer. Besides being turned into multimillion-dollar movies, Meyer's books have inspired *Twilight*-themed merchandise, including clothing, toys, and games.

In 2009 collectibles manufacturer NECA, Inc., released *Twilight* action figures. The action figures resemble characters in the *Twilight* cast, including Edward, Bella, Jacob, and Alice Cullen. The toy company Mattel, Inc., released Bella and Edward dolls in 2009, as a part of its popular Barbie series.

In October 2009, Summit Entertainment, in partnership with the Nordstrom department stores, released a clothing line that reflects the "mood and spirit of the [*Twilight*] films." Meyer also teamed with the Hobo Skate Company to produce *The Host* skateboards and T-shirts. "[Meyer's] global popularity... gives us a huge boost in selling products that will contribute to our cause," said company founder, Jared Hancock. "A portion of all sales will go to the Hobo Founda-

***Twilight* toy:** Bella and other characters from the *Twilight* movies have been made into action figures.

tion to help homeless families."

Not everyone sees Meyer's venture into merchandising and fashion as a positive thing. One MTV.com user posted the comment, "I love her books... but this is too much," she wrote. "Now everybody can be a designer... OMG!!... what is next?"

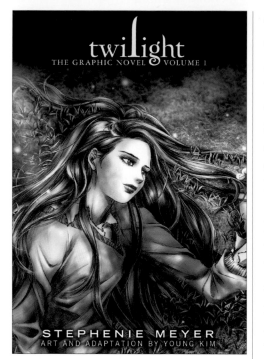

Graphic novel: Meyer collaborated with artist Young Kim to produce a graphic novel of *Twilight*.

Though Meyer didn't write the dialogue for the book, she did insist on reviewing the final draft. She requested that particular scenes be included in the book. She also tweaked some of the dialogue to sound more like her characters.

In March 2010, Yen Press released the first volume in the two-volume *Twilight* graphic novel series—with a whopping first-run printing of 350,000 copies. Meyer was thrilled with the project's outcome. "For me, it takes me back to the days when I was writing *Twilight*. It's been a while since I was really able to read *Twilight*; there is so much baggage attached to that book for me now. It seems like all I can see are the mistakes in the writing," Meyer told *Entertainment Weekly*. "Reading Young's version brought me back to the feeling I had when I was writing and it was just me and the characters again. I love that. I thank her for it."

Despite her many creative projects, roles that pull her in different directions, and her "literary rock star" status, Meyer remains centered.

The Twilight Saga: Eclipse debuted in theaters in June 2010. Actors Kristen Stewart, Robert Pattinson, and Taylor Lautner returned as Bella, Edward, and Jacob.

"The nice thing is that 95% of the time, I'm just Mom . . . and I'm here, and it's good," Meyer told *USA Today*.

Both sincere and modest, Meyer sometimes still has a hard time believing in her success. When she sees her thick books on bookstore shelves, she can hardly believe it. "I'm living the dream," says Meyer. "I feel like I've been blessed, like this is what I was supposed to be doing and I had a lot of help from the outside. I was guided, in a way, to get here."

To her many readers, Meyer is a beloved author. Her fans include one of her all-time favorite writers, Orson Scott Card. "[Stephenie Meyer] writes with luminous clarity, never standing between the reader and the dream they share," said Card. "She's the real thing."

Fans of *Twilight* were delighted when Stephenie Meyer released another vampire tale in June 2010. *The Short Second Life of Bree Tanner: An Eclipse Novella* tells the story of Bree, a teenage girl newly made into a vampire. Readers learned of Bree in *Eclipse*. As a special gift to her fans, Meyer released a free online version of *Bree Tanner* between June 7 and July 5, 2010, on her official website.

Meyer's biggest gift is her ability to engulf a reader in a story. "I've never read a book where I felt like I wasn't reading it," said a female fan. "I felt like I was right there, inside the book."

Fortunately for her fans, Stephenie Meyer enjoys writing just as much as they like reading her books. "Once I unlocked the door," says Meyer of her 2003 dream of *Twilight*, "there were a lot of stories waiting to get out."

TIMELINE

1973   Stephenie Morgan is born in Hartford, Connecticut.

1977   The Morgan family moves to Scottsdale, Arizona, a suburb of Phoenix.

1987   Stephenie begins high school at Chaparral High School in Scottsdale.

1991   Stephenie wins a scholarship to Brigham Young University, in Provo, Utah.

1993   Stephenie gets to know a childhood acquaintance, Christian "Pancho" Meyer.

Meyer in high school

1994   Morgan and Meyer marry.

1995   Stephenie Meyer graduates from Brigham Young University with a degree in English. She takes a job as a receptionist at a real estate office.

Meyer was a stay-at-home mom when she began writing.

1997 The Meyers' first son, Gabriel, is born. Meyer quits her office job to be a stay-at-home mother.

2000 The Meyers' second son, Seth, is born.

2002 The Meyers' third son, Eli, is born.

2003 Meyer has a vivid dream that inspires her to begin writing the *Twilight* story. She finishes writing the story in two months and begins sending it to literary agents. By the end of the year, Meyer signs a three-book deal with Little, Brown Books for Young Readers.

2004 Meyer writes the *Twilight* sequel *New Moon*.

2005 Meyer's first book, *Twilight*, is published and secures a spot on a *New York Times* best seller list.

Meyer signs an autograph for a fan.

2006 *New Moon* is released.

2007 *Eclipse*, the third book in the *Twilight* series, sells 150,000 copies within twenty-four hours of its release.

Meyer promoting *The Host*

2008   Meyer releases her first science fiction novel, *The Host*. Little, Brown releases the fourth *Twilight* book, *Breaking Dawn*. The movie version of *Twilight* premieres.

2009   *Twilight* and its sequels take the top four spots on *USA Today*'s Top 100 Books of 2008 list. The newspaper names Meyer its Author of the Year. *The Twilight Saga: New Moon* opens in theaters worldwide. Nordstrom department stores and other companies begin selling *Twilight*-themed clothes, dolls, and skateboards.

Pancho and Stephenie Meyer

2010   Yen Press releases a graphic novel version of *Twilight*. *The Twilight Saga: Eclipse* opens in theaters worldwide. *The Short Second Life of Bree Tanner: An Eclipse Novella* is released.

GLOSSARY

advance: an arrangement in which a publisher pays an author a certain amount of money upfront, before a book is published and sold

Barbie: a doll first launched in the United States in 1959. Special edition Barbie dolls often follow popular culture trends—such as the *Twilight*-themed Barbies released in 2009.

best seller lists: lists published by newspapers and magazines detailing the top-selling books in a given period. Some large periodicals, such as the *New York Times*, have several lists in different categories (fiction, nonfiction, children's books, and the like). Periodicals develop their lists by gathering sales figures from bookstores and book wholesalers (companies that sell books to retail stores).

book signing: a scheduled public appearance at which an author autographs books and speaks to fans

box office: a term that reflects the ticket sales of movies. Box office numbers are used to measure the popular and financial success of a movie.

Dracula: a famous literary and movie vampire first introduced in the 1897 novel *Dracula* by Bram Stoker

Facebook: a website that allows users to create personal profiles, communicate with friends, and join networks of people with common interests

genre: a category of literature (or other art form) typified by a particular style or subject matter. Vampire fiction, science fiction, horror, and romance are examples of genres.

literary agent: someone who represents an author's legal and financial interests and helps the author secure a contract with a publisher

manuscript: an unpublished piece of writing

Mormon: belonging to the Christian sect founded by Joseph Smith Jr. in New York State in 1830. Many Mormons are members of the Church of Jesus Christ of Latter-day Saints (LDS).

premiere: the first showing of a new movie at a theater

publisher: a person or company that prepares and produces a work (such as a book, a newspaper, or music) for sale and distribution

Quileute: a Native American nation of the U.S. Pacific Northwest

rejection letter: a letter from an editor or publisher informing an author that the publishing company will not publish the author's manuscript

release: the date a book, a movie, or a DVD is available for sale to the public

reviewer: a person who evaluates a work, such as a book or a movie, and writes a published opinion on the work

saga: a long and detailed story

sequel: a book or other work that continues the story told in an earlier work

vampire: a legendary creature that feeds on the blood of humans. In most Western tales, a normal human transforms into a vampire after being bitten by another vampire.

werewolf: in legends a human who transforms into a wolf

young adult (YA): a book-publishing category that focuses on readers twelve to eighteen years old

SOURCE NOTES

7–8 Natasha F., e-mail interview with author, November 24, 2009.

8 Christine, e-mail interview with author, November 16, 2009.

8–9 Deborah Brady, telephone interview with author, October 7, 2009.

9 Stephenie Meyer, interview by Oprah Winfrey, *The Oprah Winfrey Show*, November 13, 2009.

9 Natasha F.

9 Alesha Lurie, telephone interview with author, December 1, 2009.

9 Stephenie Meyer, *AuthorsReading.com*, n.d., http://authorsreading.com (February 25, 2010).

13 Gillian Cumming, "Into the Night," *Sunday Mail* (Brisbane), April 19, 2009.

15 Stephenie Meyer, *Book Lust with Nancy Pearl*, podcast interview, December 8, 2007, http://www.seattlechannel.org/podcasts/BookLust.xml (April 7, 2010).

17 Karen Valby, "Stephenie Meyer: 12 of My 'Twilight' Inspirations," *Entertainment Weekly*, November 5, 2008, http://www.ew.com/ew/gallery/0,,20234559_20234565_20237747,00.html (September 14, 2009).

18 Ibid.

19 Lev Grossman, "The Next J.K. Rowling?" *Time*, May 5, 2008, 49.

25 Tony Allen-Mills, "Her Vampire's Right Behind You, JK; Interview," *Sunday Times* (London), August 10, 2008, 5.

25 Meyer, *Book Lust*.

27 Jay Dixit, "Night School: A Hundred Years after Freud. One Man May Have Figured Out Why We Dream. You'll Never Think the Same Way about Nightmares Again," *Psychology Today*, June 2007, 88.

27 Lev Grossman, "It's Twilight in America," *Time*, November 23, 2009, 52.

28 Damian Whitworth, "Harry Who? Meet the New J.K. Rowling." *Times* (London), May 13, 2008.

29 Meyer, Oprah Winfrey interview.

29 Meyer, *Book Lust*.

30 Rick Margolis, "Love at First Bite," *School Library Journal*, October 2005, 37.

32–33 Whitworth.

34   *Time*, "10 Questions (Stephenie Meyer)," September 1, 2008, 4.

34   Stephenie Meyer, interview by Ellen DeGeneres, *The Ellen DeGeneres Show*, NBC, September 17, 2008.

35   Valby.

35   Whitworth.

35   Meyer, Oprah Winfrey interview.

35   Meyer, *Book Lust*.

40   Meyer, Ellen DeGeneres interview.

40   Allen-Mills.

41   Meyer, *Book Lust*.

41–42   Stephenie Meyer, Stephenie Meyer's Official Website, August 28, 2008, http:www.stepheniemeyer.com (October 24, 2009).

42   Meyer, Ellen DeGeneres interview.

44   Meyer, Stephenie Meyer's Official Website.

45   Ibid.

46   Grossman, "It's Twilight in America."

47   Karen Valby and Kate Ward, "The Vampire Empire," *Entertainment Weekly*, July 18, 2008, 22.

51   Valby.

51   Ibid.

51   Meyer, Oprah Winfrey interview.

52   Carol Memmott, "*Twilight* Author Stephenie Meyer Unfazed as Fame Dawns," *USA Today*, July 31, 2008, 01D.

53   Hillias J. Martin. "Stephenie Meyer: *Twilight*." *School Library Journal*, October 2005, 166.

53   Grossman, "The Next J.K. Rowling?"

53   Jo De Guia, "Stephenie Meyer: *Twilight* (I'm Not Loving.)" *Bookseller*, May 1, 2009, 13.

53   Laura Yao, "Bitten and Smitten," *Washington Post*, August 1, 2008, C01.

54   Ibid.

54   Whitworth.

54   Brady.

54   Ibid.

55   Ibid.

55   *Time*, "10 Questions.

55   Grossman, "The Next J.K. Rowling?"

56 Grossman, "It's Twilight in America."

56 Allen-Mills.

57 Whitworth.

57 Stephenie Meyer, "Q+A in Burlington, VT," YouTube, KristinaJean84, September 2007, http://www.youtube.com/user/KristinaJean84 (October 2, 2009).

59 Laura Whitcomb, Stephenie Meyer, A. M. Jenkins, and Melissa de la Cruz, "Ghosts and Vampires: What's the YA Attraction?" panel discussion, Texas Library Association, April 12, 2007, available online at http://www.youtube.com/watch?v=aXc58tIfhP8 (October 2, 2009).

60 Valby and Ward.

60 Bob Meadows and Kari Lydersen, "Stephenie Meyer Written in Blood," *People Weekly*, September 8, 2008, 90.

61 Valby and Ward.

61 Memmott.

62 Stephenie Meyer. "Q&A in San Francisco," YouTube, posted by VideoCecilia, February 2, 2009, http://www.youtube.com/watch?v=UCxyMprxsno (September 29, 2009).

62 Ibid.

62 Whitcomb, Meyer, Jenkins, and de la Cruz, panel discussion.

63 Twilight Lexicon website, posted by pelirroja, June 3, 2008, http://www.twilightlexicon.com/?p=645 (October 3, 2009).

63 Ibid.

67 Meadows and Lydersen.

67 Lurie.

67 Ibid.

68 Whitworth.

69 Richard Corliss, "Opposites Attract," *Time*, December 1, 2008, 77.

69 Stephenie Meyer, "Stephenie's Answers," The Twilight Saga, http://www.thetwilightsaga.com/page/stephenie-meyer-answers-your (November 10, 2009).

70 Ibid.

70 Ibid.

70 Ibid.

71 Christine, November 22, 2009.

71 Lurie.

71–72 Ann Shubert, telephone interview with author, August 24, 2009.

72 Martin Romero, e-mail interview with author, November 13, 2009.

72 Ibid.

73 Grossman, "The Next J.K. Rowling?"

73 Whitworth.

74 Jan D., e-mail interview with author, November 15, 2009.

74 Lurie.

74 Lorrie Lynch, "Stephen King on J.K. Rowling, Stephenie Meyer," The Who's News Blog, *USA Weekend*, February 2, 2009, http://blogs.usaweekend.com/whos_news/2009/02/exclusive-steph.html (October 23, 2009).

74 Alison Flood, "Twilight Author Stephenie Meyer 'Can't Write Worth a Darn', says Stephen King," guardian.co.uk, February 5, 2009, http://www.guardian.co.uk/books/2009/feb/05/stephenking-fiction (October 23, 2009).

76 Hannah Howard, e-mail interview with author, November 16, 2009.

76 Ibid.

76 Paige Dickerson. "Forks, Port Angeles Eateries Set the Table with Twilight-Inspired Food," *Peninsula Daily News*, August 1, 2008, http://www.peninsuladailynews.com (November 3, 2009).

76 Ibid.

77 Howard.

77 Jennie Yabroff, "Why Is It a Sin to Read for Fun?" *Newsweek*, April 20, 2009, 60.

78 Natasha F.

78 Ibid.

79 Christine, November 16, 2009.

79 Ibid.

79 United Press International, "Meyer Scraps New Book after Internet Leak," UPI.com, September 2, 2008, http://www.upi.com/Entertainment_News/2008/09/02/Meyer-scraps-new-book-after-Internet-leak/UPI-96181220369257 (February 25, 2010).

81 "Stephenie Meyer: Twitter Twits Ruin the Fun for Twilight Author," ContactMusic.com, June 29, 2009, http://www.contactmusic.com/news.nsf/story/twitter-twits-ruin-the-fun-for-twilight-writer_1105892 (October 23, 2009).

81 Ibid.

81 *Newsweek*, "The Secret Life of Vampires," August 4, 2008, 63.

82–83 Lurie.

83 Mara Reinstein, "Stop the Twilight Insanity!" *Huffington Post*, November 21, 2009, http://www.huffingtonpost.com/mara-reinstein/stop-the-twilight-insanit_b_366467.html (November 22, 2009).

83 Nancy Gibbs, "New Moon Review: Team Jacob Ascending," *Time*, November 19, 2009, http://www.time.com/time/printout/0,8816,1941094,00.html (November 22, 2009).

85 Christine, November 16, 2009.

86 Gibbs.

87 88 Christine, Novmeber 22, 2009.

88 Meyer, "Stephenie's Answers."

88 Lurie, telephone interview.

89 Jaimee Rose, "Queen of the Vampires," *Arizona Republic*, November 9, 2007, http://www.azcentral.com/ent/movies/articles/2007/11/09/20071109stepheniemeyer1110.html (February 24, 2010).

89 Memmott.

90 Stephenie Meyer, interview by Chris Cuomo, *Good Morning America*, ABC, July 31, 2008.

90 Robert Sullivan, "Dreamcatcher: Stephenie Meyer and Her Writing of *Twilight*," *Vogue*, March 2009, 448.

90 Meyer, Chris Cuomo interview.

91 Valby.

91 Sullivan.

91 Valby.

91 Meyer, *Book Lust*.

93 United Press International, "Nordstrom to Sell 'Twilight' Clothing Line," UPI.com, July 23, 2009, http://www.upi.com/Entertainment_News/2009/07/23/Nordstrom-to-sell-Twilight-clothing-line/UPI-36251248364265 (February 25, 2010).

93 Terri Schwartz, "'Twilight' Author Stephenie Meyer Gets Her Own Clothingline!" MTV.com, Hollywood Crush, September 2, 2009, http://hollywoodcrush.mtv.com/2009/09/02/twilight-author-stephenie-meyer-gets-her-own-clothingline (September 29, 2009).

93 Ibid.

94   Tina Jordan, "Exclusive: *Twilight*, the Graphic Novel," EW.com, EW's Shelf Life, January 20, 2010, http://shelf-life.ew.com/2010/01/20/exclusive-twilight-the-graphic-novel (February 24, 2010).

94   Memmott.

94–95 Rose.

95   Orson Scott Card, "Stephenie Meyer," Time.com, April 30, 2008, http://www.time.com/time/specials/2007/article/0,28804,1733748_1733752_1736282,00.html (September 29, 2009).

95   Lurie.

95   *Time*, "10 Questions."

SELECTED BIBLIOGRAPHY

Card, Orson Scott. "Stephenie Meyer." Time.com. April
    30, 2008. http://www.time.com/time/specials/2007/
    article/0,28804,1733748_1733752_1736282,00.html (September 29,
    2009).

Grossman, Lev. "It's Twilight in America." *Time*, November 23, 2009, 52.

Meyer, Stephenie. *Book Lust with Nancy Pearl*. Podcast interview, December
    8, 2007. http://www.seattlechannel.org/podcasts/BookLust.xml (April 7,
    2010).

——. Interview, CNN Newsroom, August 21, 2008. http://transcripts.cnn
    .com/TRANSCRIPTS/0808/21/cnr.04.html (March 31, 2010).

——. Interview by Chris Cuomo. *Good Morning America*, ABC, July 31, 2008.

Pham, Thailan. "Ordinary Mom by Day . . . " *People*, August 20, 2007, 47.

Rose, Jaimee. "Queen of the Vampires." *Arizona Republic*, November 9, 2007.
    http://www.azcentral.com/ent/movies/articles/2007/11/09/
    20071109stepheniemeyer1110.html (February 25, 2010).

Sirota, Peggy. "The Twilight Zone." *Vanity Fair*, December 2008,
    290. Available online at http://blogs.phoenixnewtimes.com/
    uponsun/2009/04/stephenie_meyer_js_lewis_and_m.php (September
    29, 2009).

Sullivan, Robert. "Dreamcatcher: Stephenie Meyer and Her Writing of
    Twilight." *Vogue*, March 2009, 448.

Time. "10 Questions (Stephenie Meyer)." September 1, 2008, 4.

Valby, Karen. "Stephenie Meyer." *Entertainment Weekly*, August 7, 2009, 24.

Whitcomb, Laura, Stephenie Meyer, A. M. Jenkins, and Melissa de la Cruz.
    "Ghosts and Vampires: What's the YA Attraction?" panel discussion.
    Texas Library Association, April 12, 2007. Available online at http://www
    .youtube.com/watch?v=aXc58tIfhP8 (October 2, 2009).

Whitworth, Damian. "Harry Who? Meet the New J.K. Rowling." *Times*
    (London), May 13, 2008, 4.

FURTHER READING AND WEBSITES

Allen, Amy Ruth. *Jane Austen*. Minneapolis: Twenty-First Century Books, 2001.

Gee, Joshua. *Encyclopedia Horrifica: The Terrifying TRUTH! about Vampires, Ghosts, Monsters, and More*. New York: Scholastic, 2007.

Hanley, Victoria. *Seize the Story: A Handbook for Teens Who Like to Write*. Fort Collins, CO: Cottonwood Press, 2008.

Hardwicke, Catherine. *Twilight Director's Notebook: The Story of How We Made the Movie*. New York: Little, Brown and Company, 2009.

Hopkins, Ellen, ed. *A New Dawn: Your Favorite Authors on Stephenie Meyer's Twilight Series*. Dallas: BenBella Books, 2008.

Krensky, Stephen. *Vampires*. Minneapolis: Lerner Publishing Company, 2007.

The Official Website of Stephenie Meyer
http://www.stepheniemeyer.com
Stephenie Meyer's official website contains information about Meyer's past and present projects, as well as biographical information about the author.

Sexton, Colleen. *J. K. Rowling*. Minneapolis: Twenty-First Century Books, 2008.

The Twilight Saga
http://www.thetwilightsaga.com/
This is the official online destination for fans of the *Twilight* series, sponsored by the Hachette Book Group. On the popular website, *Twilight* fans can keep up to date on new releases and upcoming *Twilight*-related projects and events.

INDEX

ABOUT THE AUTHOR

Katherine Krohn is the author of several books for young readers, including the biographies *Princess Diana, Ella Fitzgerald: First Lady of Song, Oprah Winfrey, Vera Wang,* and *Gwen Stefani.* She loves movies, feels most at home by the ocean, and does all of her writing in a vintage Airstream trailer. She lives in the Pacific Northwest with her husband, Sheggy, Lucky the dog, and their cats—Ursula, Missy, and Moon Pie.

PHOTO ACKNOWLEDGMENTS

The images in this book are used with the permission of: © Lester Cohen/
WireImage/Getty Images, p. 1; © Ingo Wagner/dpa/CORBIS, pp. 3, 48; © Rob
Schumacher/USA TODAY, pp. 4, 65, 89; © Todd Strand/Independent Picture
Service, pp. 5, 16 (top), 23 (top), 38 (top), 42, 52, 57, 64, 75 (top), 80, 84 (top),
86; © Barry King/FilmMagic/Getty Images, p. 6; © Tim Dillon/USA TODAY, p. 7;
© Steven Georges/CORBIS, p. 8; © H. Edward Kim/National Geographic/Getty
Images, p. 10; detail, portrait of Joseph Smith, Jr. © National Portrait Gallery,
Smithsonian Institution/Art Resource, NY, p. 12; © James L. Amos/National
Geographic/Getty Images, p. 13; © Bettmann/CORBIS, p. 14; © Sophie
Bassouls/Sygma/CORBIS, p. 15; © Stock Montage/Hulton Archive/Getty
Images, p. 16 (bottom); National Archives of Canada/C-011299, p. 17; Seth
Poppel Yearbook Library, pp. 19, 20, 96 (top); © Andre Jenny/Alamy, p. 21;
© Steve Granitz/WireImage/Getty Images, p. 22; © Amy Toensing/Getty
Images, p. 23 (bottom); © Summit Entertainment/Photofest, pp. 26, 31, 37,
54, 70, 88; © Emma Innocenti/Photographer's Choice RF/Getty Images, p. 29;
© Bill Hinton Photography/Flickr/Getty Images, p. 33; © Karen Shell/Polaris,
pp. 36, 41; Universal/The Kobal Collection, p. 38 (bottom); © Kevin Winter/
Getty Images, pp. 39, 71; © Basso Cannarsa/Opale/Retna Ltd., pp. 44, 96
(bottom); Photo: Surrey International Writers' Conference, p. 45; Photo by
Lee Pellegrini/Macalester Today Spring 2002, p. 46; © Mick Hutson/Redferns/
Getty Images, p. 49; © Dan MacMedan/USA TODAY, p. 50; © Eddie Malluk/
WireImage/Getty Images, p. 51; © USA TODAY, p. 55; AP Photo/Ross D.
Franklin, p. 56; f44/ZUMA Press/Newscom, pp. 58, 98 (top); © Tony Nelson/
Retna Ltd., p. 59; © Brad Barket/Getty Images, pp. 61, 63, 67; © Kevin Mazur/
TCA 2009/WireImage/Getty Images, p. 62; © RD/Leon/Retna Ltd., p. 66;
© Katy Winn/CORBIS, p. 68; Imprint Entertainment/Maverick Films/Summit
Entertainment/Newcomb, Deana/Newscom, p. 69; © Don Faust/USA TODAY,
p. 73; © Jeff Kravitz/FilmMagic/Getty Images, p. 75 (bottom); Deano/Splash
News/Newscom, p. 76; © Josh T. Reynolds/USA TODAY, p. 77; ZUMA Press/
Newscom, p. 78; © John Shearer/WireImage/Getty Images, p. 82; © Carlos
Alvarez, p. 83; © Ann Kerns, p. 84 (bottom); AP Photo/Colin Braley, p. 85;
REUTERS/Mario Anzuoni, p. 87; PacificCoastNews/Newscom, p. 90; © Jordan
Strauss/Getty Images, pp. 91, 98 (bottom); © Danita Delimont/Alamy, p. 92;
© Ruaridh Stewart/ZUMA Press, p. 93; Hachette Book Group, p. 94; © Albert
L. Ortega/WireImage/Getty Images, p. 97.

Front cover: © Katy Winn/CORBIS.
Back cover: © Rob Schumacher/USA TODAY.